The Asian World
600-1500

Teaching Guide

Oxford University Press, Inc., publishes works that
further Oxford University's objective of excellence
in research, scholarship, and education.

Oxford   New York
Auckland   Cape Town   Dar es Salaam   Hong Kong   Karachi
Kuala Lumpur   Madrid   Melbourne   Mexico City   Nairobi
New Delhi   Shanghai   Taipei   Toronto

With offices in
Argentina   Austria   Brazil   Chile   Czech Republic   France   Greece
Guatemala   Hungary   Italy   Japan   Poland   Portugal   Singapore
South Korea   Switzerland   Thailand   Turkey   Ukraine   Vietnam

Copyright © 2005 by Oxford University Press

Published by Oxford University Press, Inc.
198 Madison Avenue, New York, NY, 10016
www.oup.com

Oxford is a registered trademark of Oxford University Press

All rights reserved. No part of this publication may be reproduced,
stored in a retrieval system, or transmitted, in any form or by any means,
electronic, mechanical, photocopying, recording, or otherwise,
without the prior permission of Oxford University Press.

ISBN-13: 978-0-19-522256-2 (California edition)   ISBN-13: 978-0-19-522347-7

Writers: Erin Cleary, Sarah Jo Schwartz
          Morrison BookWorks
Project Director: Jacqueline A. Ball
Education Consultant: Diane L. Brooks, Ed.D.
Editor: Lelia Mander
Design: designlabnyc

Casper Grathwohl, Publisher

Printed in the United States of America
on acid-free paper

THE ASIAN WORLD, 600-1500
FILMS AND DOCUMENTARIES

Consider using the following films, videos, and DVDs to stimulate student interest in the subject or for extension and enrichment. Teachers should preview all films and be aware that like historical fiction, films are not always accurate in details.

China's Forbidden City (The History Channel, "In Search of History" series), available on VHS. This documentary goes inside the grand palaces, temples, libraries and theatres of the 250-acre walled city, tracing its fascinating history.

Confucius: Words of Wisdom (Biography), available on DVD and VHS. Travel to China's troubled feudal era to learn Confucius's dramatic story, from his childhood in poverty and his long road to enlightenment to his years as a celebrated teacher.

The Great Wall of China (The History Channel, "Modern Marvels" series), available on DVD and VHS. Investigate the incredible origins of the only man-made structure visible from space, and walk along the 2,000 year old barrier.

Japan: Memoirs of a Secret Empire (PBS Home Video, "Empires" series), available on DVD and VHS. Japan blossomed into its Renaissance at approximately the same time as Europe. Unlike the West, it flourished not through conquest and exploration, but by fierce and defiant isolation. This period is explored through myriad voices—the Shogun, the Samurai, the Geisha, the poet, the peasant and the Westerner who glimpsed into this secret world.

Lost Treasures of Tibet (NOVA), available on VHS. Travel to a remote part of the world for a remarkably rare look at the spectacular art created by a clandestine Buddhist culture. See astonishingly intricate and expressive Medieval wall paintings, woodcarvings, and a gravity-defying monastery built atop a cliff.

Mulan (Disney, 1998), available on DVD and VHS. This retelling of the old Chinese folktale is about the story of a young Chinese maiden who learns that her weakened and lame father is to be called up into the army in order to fight the invading Huns; she disguises herself and joins in his place.

The Silk Road (PBS, 3 volumes), available on DVD and VHS. A panoramic tour examining the world's most historic and inaccessible locations, *The Silk Road* escorts you on the legendary path traveled by Marco Polo that linked the riches of China with the European markets of the Middle Ages.

Tales of the Gun: Guns of the Orient (The History Channel), available on VHS, explores the history of weapons produced in places like China, Turkey and India, testifying to a long history and an incredible range of weapons that reflect the diversity and creativity of Eastern civilizations.

CONTENTS

Note to the Teacher   5

The Medieval & Early Modern World Program   6
    Using the Teaching Guide and Student Study Guide

Improving Literacy with *The Medieval & Early Modern World*   16

Group Projects   20

Teaching Strategies for *The Asian World, 600–1500*
    Chapter 1   Two Teachers: Buddha, Kongzi, and Early India and China   26
    Chapter 2   China United, Again: The Sui and Tang Dynasties   32
    Chapter 3   Rajas and Sultans: The Struggle for India   38
    Chapter 4   Trade if by Land and Trade if by Sea: Merchants, Religion, and Ideas   44
    Chapter 5   Bones and Buddhists: Early Korea and Japan   50
    Chapter 6   Horsemen and Gentlemen: The Song Dynasty in China   56
    Chapter 7   Khans and Conquest: The Mongol Empire   62
    Chapter 8   Sultans, Slaves, and Southerners: The Sultanate of Delhi in India   68
    Chapter 9   Khan and Emperor: The Yuan Dynasty in China   74
    Chapter 10   Warriors Rule: Kamakura and Ashikaga Japan   80
    Chapter 11   Fresh Dawn: Koryo and Early Choson Korea   86
    Chapter 12   Rise and Shine: Rulers and Treasure Ships in Ming China   92

Wrap-Up Test   98

Rubrics   100

Graphic Organizers   104

Answer Key (Teaching Guide and Student Study Guide)   112

HISTORY FROM OXFORD UNIVERSITY PRESS

"A thoroughly researched political and cultural history... makes for a solid resource for any collection."
– School Library Journal

THE WORLD IN ANCIENT TIMES
RONALD MELLOR AND AMANDA H. PODANY, EDS.
THE EARLY HUMAN WORLD
THE ANCIENT NEAR EASTERN WORLD
THE ANCIENT EGYPTIAN WORLD
THE ANCIENT SOUTH ASIAN WORLD
THE ANCIENT CHINESE WORLD
THE ANCIENT GREEK WORLD
THE ANCIENT ROMAN WORLD
THE ANCIENT AMERICAN WORLD

"Bringing history out of the Dark Ages!"

THE MEDIEVAL AND EARLY MODERN WORLD
BONNIE G. SMITH, ED.
THE EUROPEAN WORLD, 400-1450
THE AFRICAN AND MIDDLE EASTERN WORLD, 600-1500
THE ASIAN WORLD, 600-1500
AN AGE OF EMPIRES, 1200-1750
AN AGE OF VOYAGES, 1350-1600
AN AGE OF SCIENCE AND REVOLUTIONS, 1600-1800

"The liveliest, most realistic, most well-received American history series ever written for children."
– Los Angeles Times

A HISTORY OF US
JOY HAKIM
THE FIRST AMERICANS
MAKING THIRTEEEN COLONIES
FROM COLONIES TO COUNTRY
THE NEW NATION
LIBERTY FOR ALL?
WAR, TERRIBLE WAR
RECONSTRUCTING AMERICA
AN AGE OF EXTREMES
WAR, PEACE, AND ALL THAT JAZZ
ALL THE PEOPLE

FOR MORE INFORMATION, VISIT US AT WWW.OUP.COM

New from Oxford University Press
Reading History, by Janet Allen
ISBN 0-19-516595-0 hc 0-19-516596-9 pb

"*Reading History* is a great idea. I highly recommend this book."
–Dennis Denenberg, *Professor of Elementary and Early Childhood Education, Millersville University*

NOTE TO THE TEACHER

Dear Fellow Educator:

How do we realize our hopes and dreams? How do we face the challenges of everyday life? Everyone—old and young alike—asks such questions at one time or another. One place to look for answers is in the lives of people in the past. In history we find ordinary people building cathedrals and mosques, conducting trade over thousands of miles, eking out a living through agriculture and crafts, and dreaming dreams of creating vast empires. This series brings you their stories.

As educators, we want to present these stories as part of a living past—and the authors of our books aim to provide you with the materials to do just that. We offer ways to make the past come alive with vivid images in full color, lively accounts of actual people, and maps to show young readers where these people lived and how they traveled the world. Heroes tell us in their own words of their noblest hopes; villains show us their cruelty. Ordinary folks face the plague and young boys set out in creaky ships on dangerous seas. This series helps you show young adults the fullness of the past and the grand achievements that make up our heritage.

We all know that our task does not stop at presenting the *story* of the past. We must also teach our students the *skills* vital to understanding history and to becoming informed citizens. These books are designed to help you train students to think critically about human opinions, prejudices, and programs for the future. The many voices from historical actors in the series provide opportunities for students to come to terms with burning issues of bias and point of view.

You and I share not only great hopes for the future but also the daily challenges of teaching. In addition to the stories, images, quotes, maps, timelines, and young adult bibliographies of the books themselves, the series includes instructional guides with tested ideas for teaching the medieval and early modern world. These guides are filled with exercises, classroom activities, and daily lessons based on specific chapters in each book. They show additional, practical ways to make critical thinking an integral part of your work in world history.

The authors of the student books and the supporting instructional materials bring you and your students the very latest thinking about what world history is. We urge you to tell us how their presentation of this vital, emerging field works with your students. Good history, like the creation of civilization itself, depends on our common effort!

Bonnie G. Smith
General Editor

THE MEDIEVAL & EARLY MODERN WORLD PROGRAM

I. STUDENT EDITION

- Engaging, friendly narrative
- A wide range of primary sources in every chapter
- The authority of Oxford scholarship
- Period illustrations and specially commissioned maps

II. TEACHING GUIDE

- Wide range of activities and classroom approaches
- Strategies for universal access and improving literacy (ELL, struggling readers, advanced learners)
- Multiple assessment tools

III. STUDENT STUDY GUIDE

- Exercises correlated to Student Edition and Teaching Guide
- Portfolio approach
- Activities for every level of learning
- Literacy through reading and writing

PRIMARY SOURCES AND REFERENCE VOLUME

- Broad selection of primary sources in each subject area
- Ideal resource for in-class exercises and unit projects

TEACHING GUIDE: KEY FEATURES

The Teaching Guides organize each *Medieval & Early Modern World* book into chapter-based lessons of six (6) pages each, preceded by a special section that includes one longer-term project per chapter. These projects are cross-curricular, designed for mixed-group participation, and suitable for a wide range of learning styles. They can be used for teacher and student self- or peer assessment with the rubrics at the back of this Teaching Guide.

GROUP PROJECTS
Engaging, creative projects for group work on a wide variety of inviting topics

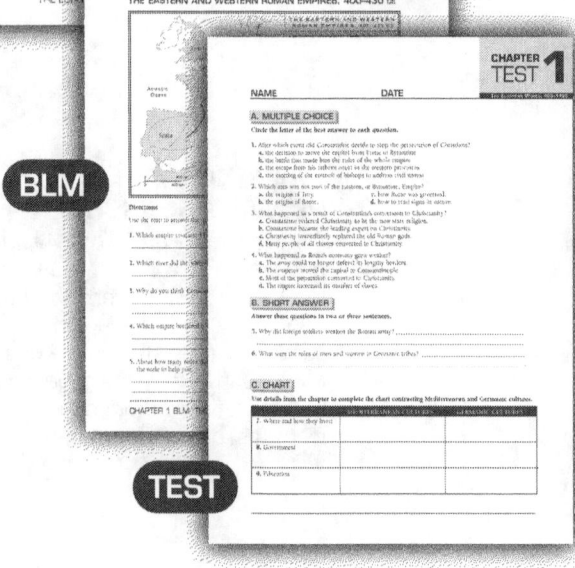

CHAPTER LESSONS
Teaching strategies and suggestions that address curriculum and that link with Student Study Guide and Student Edition

TESTS AND BLACKLINE MASTERS (BLMS)
Reproducible tests; map skills, primary sources, and document-based questions (DBQs) for assessment, homework, or classroom projects

7

TEACHING GUIDE: CHAPTER LESSONS

Teaching guides are organized so that you can easily find the information you need.

CHAPTER SUMMARY AND PERFORMANCE OBJECTIVES
The Chapter Summary gives an overview of the information in the chapter. The Performance Objectives are the three or four important goals students should achieve in the chapter. Accomplishing these goals will help students master the information in the book as well as meet standards for the course.

BUILDING BACKGROUND
This section connects students to the chapter they are about to read. Students may be asked to use what they know to make predictions about the text, preview the images in the chapter, or connect modern life with the historical subject matter.

VOCABULARY
A word list for every chapter defines difficult words and key curricular terms and recaps glossary entries.

CHAPTER 1

BELIEVERS AND BARBARIANS: THE END OF THE ROMAN EMPIRE
PAGES 20–33

FOR HOMEWORK
Student Study Guide pages 13–16
Chapter 1

CHAPTER SUMMARY
Both external and internal problems weakened Rome. When Constantine the Great converted to Christianity he moved the capital east to a city later renamed Constantinople. The empire gradually divided into the Eastern Empire and the Western Empire, each with its own version of Christianity. In 410 the Visigoths conquered Rome. However, Rome's legacy lived on through Latin, government structures, and architecture.

PERFORMANCE OBJECTIVES
▶ To identify the factors that threatened the Roman Empire
▶ To define and evaluate the key events in the life and rule of Constantine
▶ To identify the lasting contributions of Rome

BUILDING BACKGROUND
Ask students to preview the chapter by reading the headings and subheadings, studying the photographs and captions, and examining the map. Based on the preview, work with students to compile a list of questions about the fall of Rome and the rise of Christianity. As students locate the answers to their questions, have them record them on the list.

VOCABULARY
empire huge region of varied cultures under the control of one government
citizen person owing loyalty to and entitled to protection by a state or a nation
Christianity the religion based on the life and teachings of Jesus Christ
convert person who has been convinced to change from one religion to another
barbarian name given to outsiders by the Romans, who viewed them as uncivilized
drought a long period of very low rainfall
As needed, have students consult the glossary to define the following words: *bishop, centralize, council, excommunicate, heretic, New Testament, persecution, plunder, saint*

CAST OF CHARACTERS
Augustine (aw-GUS-teen), Roman nobleman who converted to Christianity
Constantine the Great (KON-stun-teen), First Roman emperor to convert to Christianity
Visigoths (VIH-zih-goths), Arian Christian Germanic tribe that attacked Rome in 410

WORKING WITH PRIMARY SOURCES
Point out the quotation from Ambrose in Student Edition page 23. If necessary, refer students to the glossary, and explain that excommunicated means to be deprived of the right of church membership by the church leadership. Discuss what the quotation reveals about early Christian beliefs. Why do you think Ambrose asked the emperor to repent? Invite students to read more of Ambrose's letter to the emperor, written in 390, at http://www.fordham.edu/halsall/source/ambrose-let51.html.

28 / CHAPTER 1

WORKING WITH PRIMARY SOURCES
A major feature of *The Medieval & Early Modern World* is the opportunity to read about history through the words and images of the people who lived it. Each book includes excerpts from the best sources from these ancient civilizations, giving the narrative an immediacy that is difficult to match in secondary sources. Students can read further in these sources on their own or in small groups using the accompanying *Primary Sources and Reference Volume*. The Teaching Guide recommends activities so students of all skill levels can appreciate the ways people from the past saw themselves, their ideas and values, and their fears and dreams.

LINKING DISCIPLINES

Art Have students research examples of arches, roads, and aqueducts constructed throughout the Roman Empire. You might want to display a map of the Roman Empire on the wall. Instruct students to research in a library or on the Internet to find examples of Roman architecture. Have them sketch or print copies, write brief captions, and affix them on the map. Ask students to identify similarities between these ancient structures and familiar modern structures.

LITERACY TIPS

In addition to using the suggestions in the Supporting Learning and Extending Learning sections, refer back frequently to pages 20–23 for strategies and advice from a literacy coach.

WRITING

Persuasive Letter Have students review the events of Augustine's life as described in the chapter. Next have them write a persuasive letter or sermon that he might have addressed to non-Christians to describe his conversion and persuade them of his beliefs. What figurative language might he use to compel them? What experiences would he share from his life? (*Assessment: students incorporate supporting detail and language from the chapter. Their letters should also represent the tensions between Christians and non-Christians.*)

SUPPORTING LEARNING

English Language Learners Help students recognize and use mu... meaning words. Using the paragraphs on Student Edition page 27, identif... define such words as letters, beat, torn, and passage. Help students use conte... clues and their prior knowledge to figure out which meaning is being used. A... volunteers to suggest sentences using various meanings of the words.

Struggling Readers Have students complete the Sequence of Events Ch... at the back of the guide to show how one event led to an...ther, and then anot... in the history of early Christianity. For example, they ...an list how Christianit... spread led to the executions of Christians, and so o... Remind them to look f... key dates, such as Constantine's conversion in 3...2.

EXTENDING LEARNING

Enrichment Invite students to learn more about one of these cities as they are today: Rome, Carthage, or Constantinople. Direct students to use search engines...

GEOGRAPHY CONNECTION

Movement Have students trace the routes of the ...rmanic migrations on the map on page 31. They may want to compare the map with a to...raphic map of Europe to locate features, such as mountains or rivers that either blocked o... aided the movement of these peoples.

READING COMPREHENSION QUESTIONS

1. Why did economic and social conditions worsen in Rome? (*Rome depended ... slaves to produc... food. When the empire stopped expanding, it had fewer slaves do the work.*)
2. Why did Roman authorit... fear the early Christians? (*They worried about uprisings. Christianity was becom...ng popular among people who would likely rebel: the poor in cities, slaves, and so...iers.*)
3. Where did Constantine locate the new cap...tal of the empire? (*Byzantium, a small Greek city near Asia Minor*)
4. Why did the Huns migrate west? (*Drought ruined thei... pasture, and they wan... better lives for themselves.*)
5. What happened after the Visigoths advanced on Rome in 410? (*...he western emperor fled, and the Visigoths plundered Rome.*)

CRITICAL THINKING QUESTIONS

1. What does the image of the shield on Student Edition page 23 tell you about warfare during this time? (*Warfare included hand-to-hand combat. Soldiers had access to iron for added protection.*)
2. Why were the Romans, Germanic tribes, and Huns in conflict with each other? (*They wanted to either keep control of land and resources, or gain land and resource... from the other groups. They fought rather than cooperate with each other.*)
3. One Goth observer described the Huns as "small, foul, and skinny." What doe... it say about the Goths' view of the Huns during this time? (*It shows their negative opinion of the Goths.*)

SOCIAL SCIENCES

Military History Attila the Hun is still famous today for his resilience and brutality. Have students research his attack on Rome using the Internet or library resources. Next have them use their history journals to write from Attila's point of view a series of short diary entries describing his advance toward Rome.

READING AND LANGUAGE ARTS

Reading Nonfiction As students read the text, have them use the strategy ...st/group/label" to work with the vocabulary. First have them individually list ...rds that relate to different cultures or religious groups as they read. Then have ...dents form groups of three and share their lists. Next, ask the groups to ...entify and name at least five categories in which to put the words, and sort ...m into the categories to which they best belong. Finally, have each small group ...play their choices and share the reasons behind them with the class.

...sing Language Direct students' attention to the quotation from Ambrose ... page 27. Have them draw in their history journals an image it brings to mind. ... partners, students can share images and discuss why Ambrose might have ...scribed the church the way he did. Next, have partners consider what the ...ging sea" represents. As a whole class, speculate about the effect of his words ... both Christians and on non-Christians.

THE EUROPEAN WORLD, 400–1450   29

WRITING
Each chapter has a suggestion for a specific writing assignment. These assignments can help students meet state requirements in writing as well improve their skills.

SUPPORTING LEARNING AND EXTENDING LEARNING
Suggestions for students of varying abilities and learning styles: advanced learners, struggling readers, auditory/visual/tactile learners, and English language learners. These may be individual, partner, or group activities. (*For more on reading and literacy, see pp. 16–19.*)

GEOGRAPHY CONNECTION
Each chapter has a Geography Connection to strengthen students' map skills as well as their understanding of how geography affects human civilization. One of the five themes of geography is highlighted in each chapter.

READING COMPREHENSION AND CRITICAL THINKING QUESTIONS
The reading comprehension questions are general enough to allow free-flowing class or small group discussion, yet specific enough to be used for oral or written assessment of students' grasp of the important information. The critical thinking questions are intended to engage students in a deeper analysis of the text and can also be used for oral or written assessment.

SOCIAL SCIENCES ACTIVITIES
These activities connect the subject matter in the Student Edition with economics, civics, and science, technology, and society.

READING AND LANGUAGE ARTS
Some activities can facilitate the development of nonfiction reading strategies. Others help students' appreciation of fiction and poetry, focusing on word choice, description, and figurative language.

TEACHING GUIDE: CHAPTER SIDEBARS

Icons quickly help identify key concepts, facts, activities, and assessment activities in the sidebars.

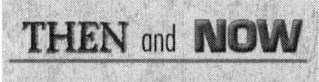

- ▶ Cast of Characters
  This sidebar points out and identifies significant personalities in the chapter. Pronunciation guides are included where necessary.

- ▶ Then and Now
  This feature provides interesting facts and ideas about the ancient civilization and relates it to the modern world. This may be an aspect of government still in use today, word origins of common modern expressions, physical reminders of the past, and other features. You can use this item simply to promote interest in the subject matter or as a springboard to other research.

- ▶ Linking Disciplines
  This feature offers opportunities to investigate other subject areas that relate to the material in the Student Edition: math, science, arts, and health. Specific areas of these subjects are emphasized: **Math** (arithmetic, algebra, geometry, data, statistics); **Science** (life science, earth science, physical science); **Arts** (music, arts, dance, drama, architecture); **Health** (personal health, world health).

- ▶ For Homework
  A quick glance links you to additional activities in the Student Study Guide that can be assigned as homework.

ASSESSMENT

The Medieval & Early Modern World program intentionally omits from the Student Edition the kinds of section, chapter, and unit questions that are used to review and assess learning in standard textbooks. It is the purpose of the series to engage readers in learning—and loving—history written as good literature. Rather than interrupting student reading and enjoyment, all assessment instruments for the series have been placed in the Teaching Guides.

▶ CHAPTER TESTS
A reproducible chapter test follows each chapter in this Teaching Guide. These tests will help you assess students' mastery of the content addressed in each chapter. These tests measure a variety of cognitive and analytical skills, particularly comprehension, critical thinking, and expository writing through multiple choice, short answer, and essay questions.
An answer key for the chapter tests is provided at the end of the Teaching Guide.

▶ WRAP-UP TEST
After the last chapter test you will find a wrap-up test consisting of 10 essay questions that evaluate students' ability to synthesize and express what they've learned about the civilization under study. Depending upon your class, you may want to consider assigning the questions as a takehome or open-book test.

▶ RUBRICS
The rubrics at the back of this Teaching Guide will help you assess students' written work, oral presentations, and group projects. They include a Scoring Rubric based on standards for good writing and effective cooperative learning. In addition, a simplified hand-out is provided, plus a form for evaluating group projects and a Library/Media Center Research Log to help students focus and evaluate their research. Students can also evaluate their own work using these rubrics.

▶ BLACKLINE MASTERS (BLMs)
Two blackline masters follow each chapter in the Teaching Guide. These BLMs are reproducible pages for you to use as in-class activities or homework exercises. Assigning primary source blackline masters to groups or partners is strongly encouraged, as this material may be quite challenging to some students. They can also be used for assessment as needed.

▶ ADDITIONAL ASSESSMENT ACTIVITIES
The Group Project sections and Chapter Lessons of this Teaching Guide provide numerous activities and projects that have been designated as additional assessment opportunities, using the rubrics at the back of this Guide.

USING THE STUDENT STUDY GUIDE FOR ASSESSMENT

▶ Study Guide Activities
Assignments in the Student Study Guide correspond with those in the Teaching Guide. If needed, these Student Study Guide activities can be used for assessment.

▶ Portfolio Approach
Student Study Guide pages can be removed from the workbook and turned in for grading. When the pages are returned, they can be part of the students' individual history journals. Have students keep a 3-ring binder portfolio of Study Guide pages alongside writing projects and other activities.

STUDENT STUDY GUIDE: KEY FEATURES

The Student Study Guide works as both standalone instructional material and as a support to the Student Edition and this Teaching Guide. Certain activities encourage informal small-group or family participation. These features make it an effective teaching tool:

Flexibility

You can use the Study Guide in the classroom, with individuals or small groups, or send it home for homework. You can distribute the entire guide to students; however, the pages are perforated so you can remove and distribute only the pertinent lessons.

A page on reports and special projects directs students to the "Further Reading" resource in the student edition. This feature gives students general guidance on doing research and devising independent study projects of their own.

FACSIMILE SPREAD
The Study Guide begins with a facsimile spread from the Student Edition. This spread gives reading strategies and highlights key features: captions, primary sources, sidebars, headings, etymologies. The spread supplies the contextualization students need to fully understand the material.

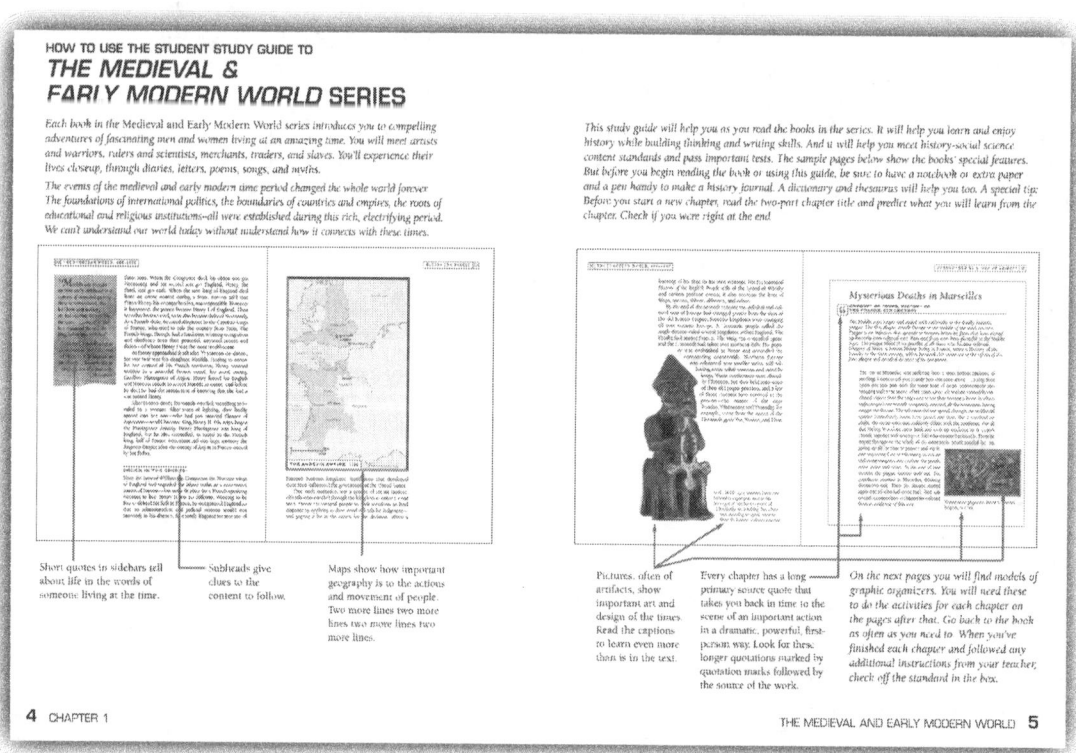

Portfolio Approach

The Study Guide pages are three-hole-punched so they can be integrated with notebook paper in a looseleaf binder. This history journal or portfolio can become both a record of content mastery and an outlet for each student's unique creative expression. Responding to prompts, students can write poetry or songs, plays and character sketches, create storyboards or cartoons, or construct multi-layered timelines.

The portfolio approach gives students unlimited opportunities for practice in areas that need strengthening. Students can share their journals and compare their work. And the Study Guide pages in the portfolio make a valuable assessment tool for you. The portfolio is an ongoing record of performance that can be reviewed and graded periodically.

> **GRAPHIC ORGANIZERS**
> This feature contains reduced models of seven graphic organizers referenced frequently in the study guide. Using these devices will help students organize the material so it is meaningful to them. (Full-size reproducibles of each graphic organizer are provided at the back of this Teaching Guide.) These graphic organizers include: outline, main idea map, K-W-L chart (What I Know, What I Want to Know, What I Learned), Venn diagram, timeline, sequence of events chart, and T-chart.

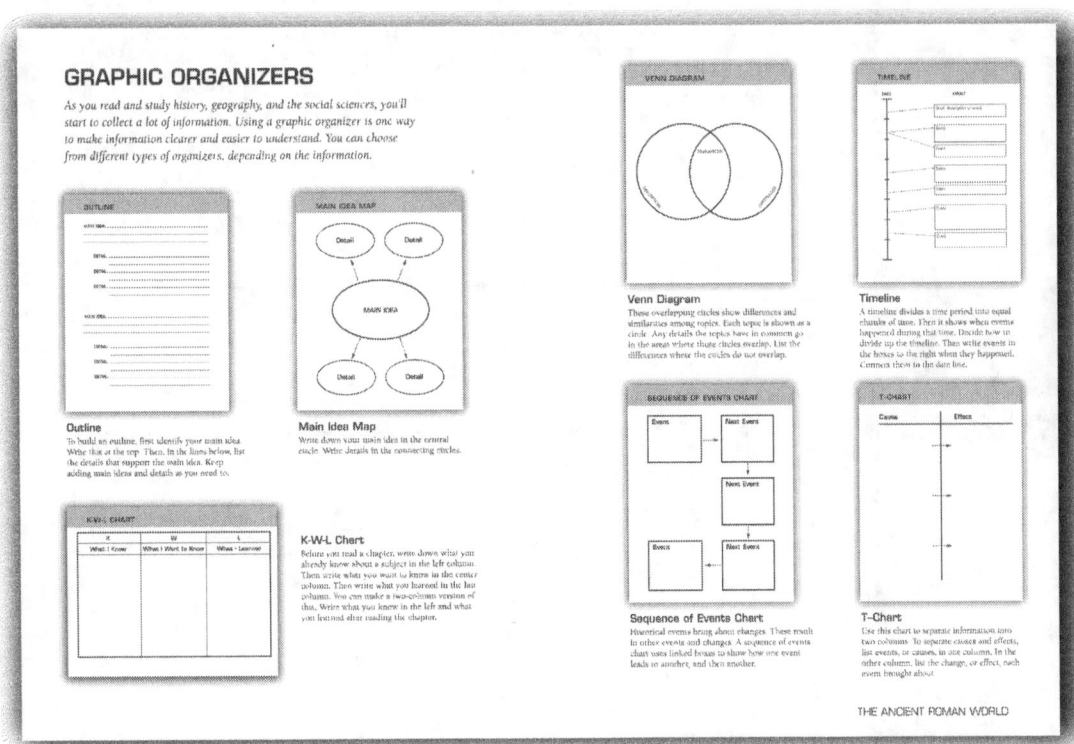

STUDENT STUDY GUIDE: CHAPTER LESSONS

Each chapter lesson is designed to draw students into the subject matter. Recurring features and exercises challenge their knowledge and allow them to practice valuable analysis and English language arts skills. Activities in the Teaching Guide and Student Study Guide complement but do not duplicate each other. Together they offer a wide range of class work, group projects, and opportunities for further study and assessment that can be tailored to all ability levels.

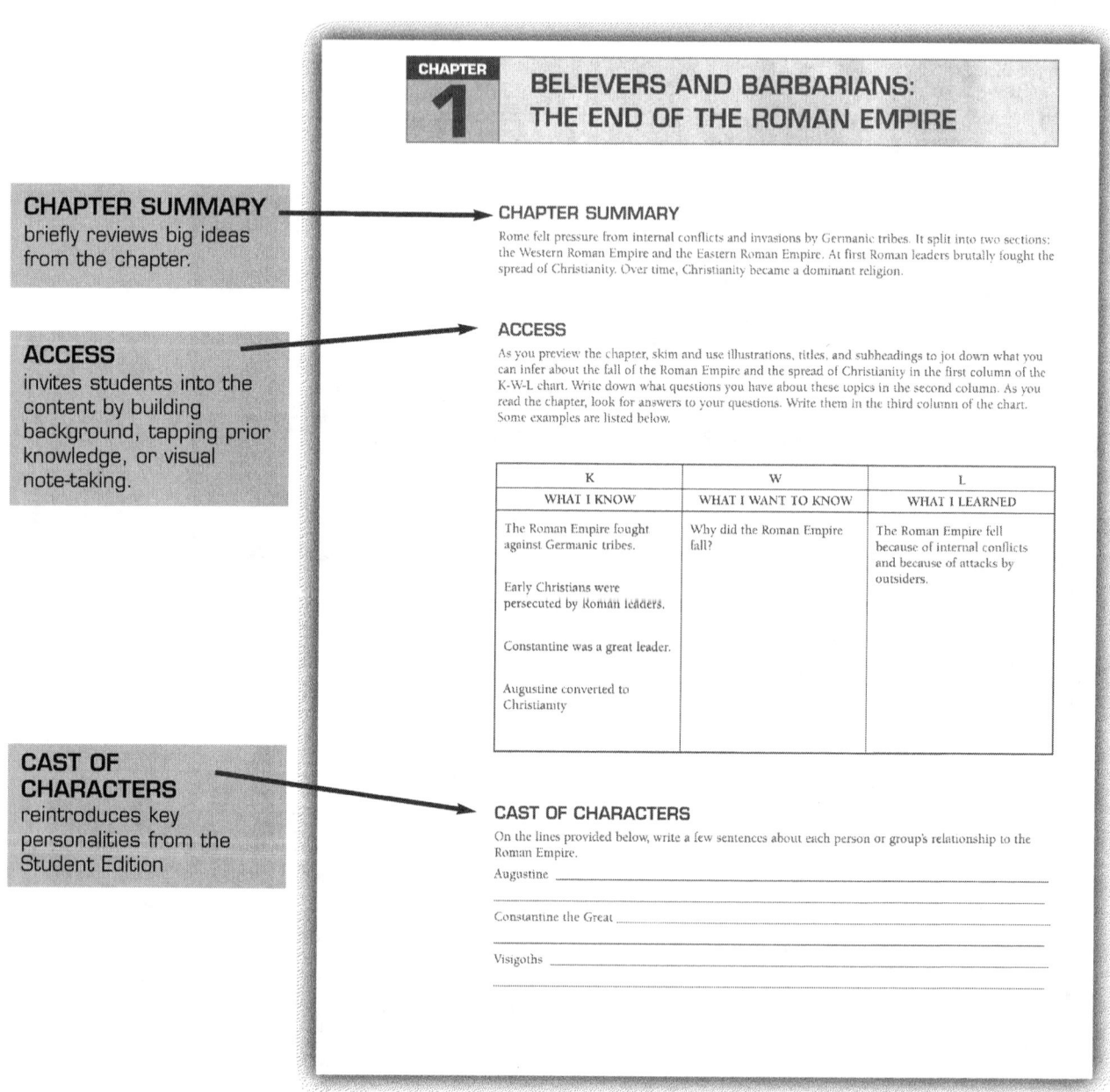

CHAPTER SUMMARY briefly reviews big ideas from the chapter.

ACCESS invites students into the content by building background, tapping prior knowledge, or visual note-taking.

CAST OF CHARACTERS reintroduces key personalities from the Student Edition

CHAPTER 1: BELIEVERS AND BARBARIANS: THE END OF THE ROMAN EMPIRE

CHAPTER SUMMARY
Rome felt pressure from internal conflicts and invasions by Germanic tribes. It split into two sections: the Western Roman Empire and the Eastern Roman Empire. At first Roman leaders brutally fought the spread of Christianity. Over time, Christianity became a dominant religion.

ACCESS
As you preview the chapter, skim and use illustrations, titles, and subheadings to jot down what you can infer about the fall of the Roman Empire and the spread of Christianity in the first column of the K-W-L chart. Write down what questions you have about these topics in the second column. As you read the chapter, look for answers to your questions. Write them in the third column of the chart. Some examples are listed below.

K WHAT I KNOW	W WHAT I WANT TO KNOW	L WHAT I LEARNED
The Roman Empire fought against Germanic tribes. Early Christians were persecuted by Roman leaders. Constantine was a great leader. Augustine converted to Christianity	Why did the Roman Empire fall?	The Roman Empire fell because of internal conflicts and because of attacks by outsiders.

CAST OF CHARACTERS
On the lines provided below, write a few sentences about each person or group's relationship to the Roman Empire.

Augustine _____

Constantine the Great _____

Visigoths _____

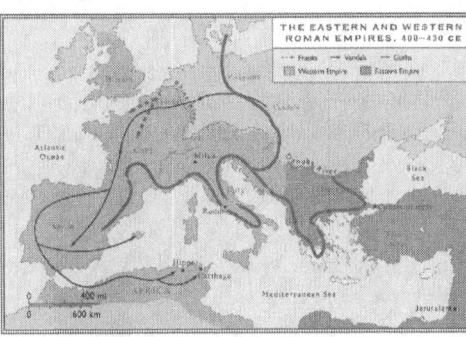

WORD BANK reintroduces key curricular terms and difficult words from the Student Edition.

CRITICAL THINKING exercises draw on such thinking skills as establishing cause and effect, making inferences, comparing and contrasting, identifying main ideas and details, and other analytical process.

WORKING WITH PRIMARY SOURCES invites students to read primary sources closely. Exercises include DBQ's, evaluating point of view, and writing.

WRITE ABOUT IT A writing assignment may stem from a vocabulary word, a historical event, or a primary source. The assignment can be a newspaper article, letter, short essay, a scene with dialogue, a diary entry.

ALL OVER THE MAP uses engaging map skills activities to help students understand geography's crucial role in shaping history.

IMPROVING LITERACY WITH THE MEDIEVAL & EARLY MODERN WORLD

The books in this series are written in a lively, narrative style to inspire a love of reading history. English language learners and struggling readers are given special consideration within the program's exercises and activities. And students who love to read and learn will also benefit from the program's rich and varied material. Following are strategies to make sure each and every student gets the most out of the subjects you will teach through *The Medieval & Early Modern World*.

ENGLISH LANGUAGE LEARNERS

For English learners to achieve academic success, the instructional considerations for teachers include two mandates:

- Help them attain grade level, content area knowledge, and academic language.
- Provide for the development of English language proficiency.

To accomplish these goals, you should plan lessons that reflect the student's level of English proficiency. Students progress through five developmental levels as they increase in language proficiency:

Beginning and Early Intermediate (*grade level material will be mostly incomprehensible, students need a great deal of teacher support*)

Intermediate (*grade level work will be a challenge*)

Early Advanced and Advanced (*close to grade level reading and writing, students continue to need support*)

Refer to your state's ELD Standards for information about language proficiency at each level. The books in this program are written at the intermediate level. However, you can still use the lesson plans for students of different levels by using the strategies below:

Tap Prior Knowledge
What students know about the topic will help determine your next steps for instruction. Using K-W-L charts, brainstorming, and making lists are ways to find out what they know. English learners bring a rich cultural diversity into the classroom. By sharing what they know, students can connect their knowledge and experiences to the course.

Set the Context
Use different tools to make new information understandable. These can be images, artifacts, maps, timelines, illustrations, charts, videos, or graphic organizers. Techniques such as role-playing and story-boarding can also be helpful. Speak in shorter sentences, with careful enunciation, expanded explanations, repetitions, and paraphrasing. Use fewer idiomatic expressions.

Show—Don't Just Tell
English learners often get lost as they listen to directions, explanations, lectures, and discussions. By showing students what is expected, you can help them participate more fully in classroom activities. Students need to be shown how to use the graphic organizers in this guide and the mini versions in the student study guide, as well as other blackline masters for note-taking and practice. An overhead transparency with whole or small groups is also effective.

Use the Text
Because of unfamiliar words, students will need help. Teach them to preview the chapter using text features (headings, bold print, sidebars, italics). See the suggestions in the facsimile of the Student Edition, shown on pages 6–7 of the Student Study Guide. Show students organizing structures such as cause and effect or comparing and contrasting. Have students read to each other in pairs. Encourage them to share their history journals with each other. Use Read Aloud/Think Aloud, perhaps with an overhead transparency. Help them create word banks, charts, and graphic organizers. Discuss the main idea after reading.

Check for Understanding
Rather than simply ask students if they understand, stop frequently and ask them to paraphrase or expand on what you just said. Such techniques will give you a much clearer assessment of their understanding.

Provide for Interaction
As students interact with the information and speak their thoughts, their content knowledge and academic language skills improve. Increase interaction in the classroom through cooperative learning, small group work, and partner share. By working and talking with others, students can practice asking and answering questions.

Use Appropriate Assessment
When modifying the instruction, you will also need to modify the assessment. Multiple choice, true and false, and other criterion reference tests are suitable, but consider changing test format and structure. English learners are constantly improving their language proficiency in their oral and written responses, but they are often grammatically incorrect. Remember to be thoughtful and fair about giving students credit for their content knowledge and use of academic language, even if their English isn't perfect.

STRUGGLING READERS

Some students struggle to understand the information presented in a textbook. The following strategies for content-area reading can help students improve their ability to make comparisons, sequence events, determine importance, summarize, evaluate, synthesize, analyze, and solve problems.

Build Knowledge of Genre
Both the fiction and narrative nonfiction genres are incorporated into *The Medieval & Early Modern World*. This combination of genres makes the text interesting and engaging. But teachers must be sure students can identify and use the organizational structures of both genres.

Fiction	Nonfiction
Each chapter is a story	Content: historical information
Setting: historical time and place	Organizational structure: cause/effect, sequence of events, problem/solution
Characters: historical figures	Other features: maps, timelines, sidebars, photographs, primary sources
Plot: problems, roadblocks, and resolutions	

In addition, the textbook has a wealth of the text features of nonfiction: bold and italic print, sidebars, headings and subheadings, labels, captions, and "signal words" such as *first*, *next*, and *finally*. Teaching these organizational structures and text features is essential for struggling readers.

Build Background

Having background information about a topic makes reading about it so much easier. When students lack background information, teachers can preteach or "front load" concepts and vocabulary, using a variety of instructional techniques. Conduct a chapter or book walk, looking at titles, headings, and other text features to develop a big picture of the content. Focus on new vocabulary words during the "walk" and create a word bank with illustrations for future reference. Read aloud key passages and discuss the meaning. Focus on the timeline and maps to help students develop a sense of time and place. Show a video, go to a website, and have trade books and magazines on the topic available for student exploration.

Comprehension Strategies

While reading, successful readers are predicting, making connections, monitoring, visualizing, questioning, inferring, and summarizing. Struggling readers have a harder time with these "in the head" processes. The following strategies will help these students construct meaning from the text until they are able to do it on their own.

>**PREDICT:** Before reading, conduct a picture and text feature "tour" of the chapter to make predictions. Ask students if they remember if this has ever happened before, to predict what might happen this time.

>**MAKE CONNECTIONS:** Help students relate content to their background (text to text, text to self, and text to the world).

>**MONITOR AND CONFIRM:** Encourage students to stop reading when they come across an unknown word, phrase, or concept. In their notebooks, have them make a note of text they don't understand and ask for clarification or figure it out. While this activity slows down reading at first, it is effective in improving skills over time.

>**VISUALIZE:** Students benefit from imagining the events described in a story. Sketching scenes, story-boarding, role-playing, and looking for sensory details all help students with this strategy.

>**INFER:** Help students look beyond the literal meaning of a text to understand deeper meanings. Graphic organizers and discussions provide opportunities to broaden their understanding. Looking closely at the "why" of historical events helps students infer.

>**QUESTION AND DISCUSS:** Have students jot down their questions as they read, and then share them during discussions. Or have students come up with the type of questions they think a teacher would ask. Over time students will develop more complex inferential questions, which lead to group discussions. Questioning and discussing also helps students see ideas from multiple perspectives and draw conclusions, both critical skills for understanding history.

DETERMINE IMPORTANCE: Teach students how to decide what is most important from all the facts and details in nonfiction. After reading for an overall understanding, they can go back to highlight important ideas, words, and phrases. Clues for determining importance include bold or italic print, signal words, and other text features. A graphic organizer such as a main idea map also helps.

Teach and Practice Decoding Strategies

Rather than simply defining an unfamiliar word, teach struggling readers decoding strategies:

- Have them look at the prefix, suffix, and root to help figure out the new word.
- Look for words they know within the word.
- Use the context for clues, and read further or reread.

ADVANCED LEARNERS

Every classroom has students who finish the required assignments and then want additional challenges. Fortunately, the very nature of history and social science offers a wide range of opportunities for students to explore topics in greater depth. Encourage them to come up with their own ideas for an additional assignment. Determine the final product, its presentation, and a timeline for completion.

▶ Research

Students can develop in-depth understanding through seeking information, exploring ideas, asking and answering questions, making judgments, considering points of view, and evaluating actions and events. They will need access to a wide range of resource materials: the Internet, maps, encyclopedias, trade books, magazines, dictionaries, artifacts, newspapers, museum catalogues, brochures, and the library. See the "Further Reading" section at the end of the Student Edition for good jumping-off points.

▶ Projects

You can encourage students to capitalize on their strengths as learners (visual, verbal, kinesthetic, or musical) or to try a new way of responding. Students can prepare a debate or write a persuasive paper, play, skit, poem, song, dance, game, puzzle, or biography. They can create an alphabet book on the topic, film a video, do a book talk, or illustrate a book. They can render charts, graphs, or other visual representations. Allow for creativity and support students' thinking.

Cheryl A. Caldera, M.A.
Literacy Coach

GROUP PROJECTS

These interactive, multimedia projects give every student the chance to experience some aspect of life in *The Asian World, 600–1500*. They will add fun and depth to your exploration of this amazing time in history and can be used for assessment with the rubrics at the back of this Teaching Guide.

Chapter 1
▶ **Read and Respond to Siddhartha by Herman Hesse**
Based on the early life of Gautama Buddha, *Siddhartha*, published in 1922, demonstrates German novelist and poet Herman Hesse's knowledge of and appreciation for Buddhism and Hinduism. Ask students to read this simple-to-read yet profound novel, and then let small groups discuss it together. Students can compare Hesse's ideas with the information they learned about Buddhism in the chapter. You may want to introduce the book by reading the first few pages aloud to the entire class and discussing them as a group before students begin reading independently. After students have read and discussed the novel, ask each student to write a personal reaction to the work. Share with the class the assessment rubric at the back of this guide.

Chapter 2
▶ **Wu Zhao: The Book Jacket**
Without a doubt, Wu Zhao, China's only woman emperor, led one of the most amazing lives of any woman in history. Let pairs of students review the information about Wu Zhao in the chapter and then discuss her life and accomplishments. Direct students to imagine that they have written a biography of Wu Zho. Have them choose an alluring title for their biography, write copy, and design art for the dust jacket of the book. Encourage them to study several jackets to figure out why some are more appealing than others and to make sure they include all the parts, including the front and back flaps. Finally, let students produce the cover, with or without the aid of a computer. Display the jackets in the classroom so that everyone can enjoy them. Share with the class the assessment rubric at the back of this guide.

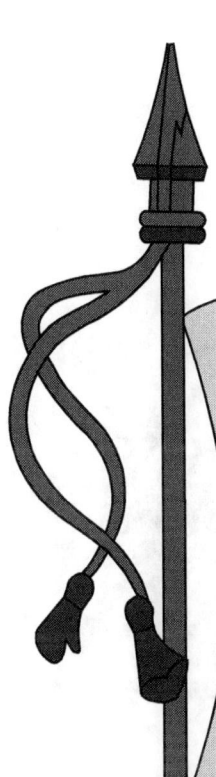

Chapter 3
▶ An Astonishing Discovery

No one knows which anonymous Indian first conceived of the concept of zero (or even whether the idea was the brainstorm of an individual or many people over time), but we do know how profoundly this idea affected world history. Ask students to imagine that they were the originator of this monumental idea. Have each student write a monologue in which he or she describes that thrilling moment. Encourage students to be as lighthearted as they wish, but to attempt to describe the importance of this idea. Have students perform their monologues for their classmates or a larger audience. Ask the audience to use the assessment rubric at the back of this guide to evaluate the performances.

Chapter 4
▶ Silk Road Itinerary

Have students take on the role of Asian travel agent in 1000 CE. Let them plan an itinerary for the six-month-long travels of a Chinese or Indian merchant along the Silk Road. Ask students to list all the stops the merchant will make and the length of time the merchant will stay in those places. Caution students to do as much research as necessary to be sure that they include only places that actually existed along the Silk Road in 1000 CE. Urge students to compare their completed itineraries. Share with the class the assessment rubric at the back of this guide.

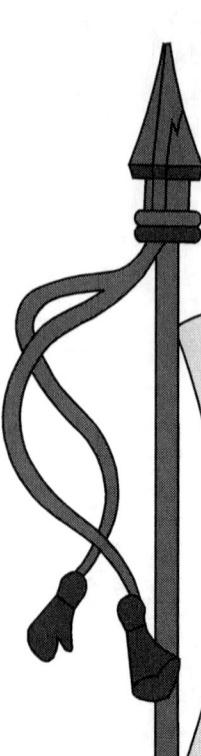

Chapter 5
▶ Hot Off the Press

Let pairs of students review the information in the chapter about either of these two notable developments: the corruption of Silla officials during the 9th century or the causes of Japan's civil wars that broke out in 1185. Then ask students to transport themselves back in time to become eyewitnesses to an event related to one of the developments, and let them work together to write news reports about it. Encourage students to combine imagination and facts and to use such contemporary features as quotations and riveting headlines. Students may wish to use desktop publishing software to produce realistic, multi-column news reports. Post completed news reports on a bulletin board. Share with the class the assessment rubric at the back of this guide.

Chapter 6
▶ Song Dynasty Poetry Reading

Have students review the information in the chapter about art, particularly poetry, during the Song Dynasty. Then have them locate several Song Dynasty poems by poets such as Li Qingzhao and choose a poem that appeals to them. During a designated period over several days, hold a Song Dynasty poetry reading, in which students read aloud or recite the poem they chose. Let the audience react to each poem and evaluate the reading or recitation using the assessment rubric at the back of this guide.

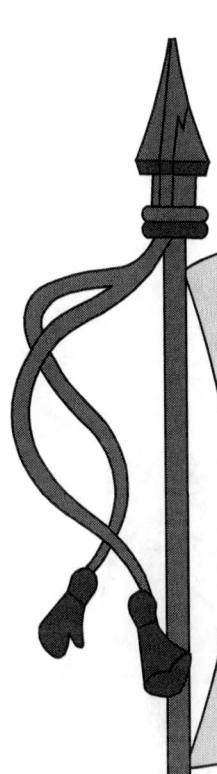

Chapter 7
▶ Mural of the Rise of Genghis Khan

No matter what one's view of Genghis Khan's tactics and behavior, he had an undeniably thrilling life and left a permanent legacy. After students review the events in Genghis Khan's early life and rise to power, let them suggest five to six dramatic scenes to depict in art. List the scenes on the board and let students choose the one they would like to illustrate. If necessary, balance the groups to make them roughly equal. Encourage groups to do as much research as they can to increase the accuracy of their illustrations. Then have each group illustrate the scene it chose on butcher paper. After the illustrations are complete, tape them together to form a mural for the classroom walls. Share with the class the assessment rubric at the back of this guide.

Chapter 8
▶ Cultural Comparison

Divide students into partnerships. Ask the partners to decide which person will research Muslim customs and which will research Hindu customs. Ask partnerships to make a list of categories to research, such as food and clothing. Then have students review the chapter as well as research at the library or on the Internet to find information about the topics they have listed. Ask students to write what they learn in their history journals. Then allow class time for partners to compare what they have discovered and organize their information onto a comparison chart. As a culminating activity, have partners give oral presentations about the customs of the two cultures. Share with the class the assessment rubric at the back of this guide.

Chapter 9
▸ On the Road with Marco Polo

Divide the class into partnerships and have them research the experience of Marco Polo in China and his travels along the Silk Road. Ask students to find as much information as they can about the relationship between Marco Polo and Khubilai Khan during Marco Polo's stay in China. Also have them research the impact Marco Polo's travels had on his native Italy when he returned. Have them keep a record of their findings in their history journals. Then ask partners to work together to write a travel journal from the perspective of Marco Polo about his experiences. Encourage students to use descriptive language in their writing. This project could culminate with partners binding their journal entries together and displaying the journals in the classroom. Class time can be provided for students to read at each other's Silk Road journals. Share with the class the assessment rubric at the back of this guide.

Chapter 10
▸ The Simple Life

Divide the class into small groups and have them study the images of the Japanese Zen arts in their books. Then have each group choose an area of the Zen arts mentioned in the chapter to research further. For homework, students can find information at the library or on the Internet about their area of Zen art and how this type of art influenced the Japanese people. Students may also need to gather props for their presentations. Each small group can give a presentation about their area of Zen art. Share with the class the assessment rubric at the back of this guide.

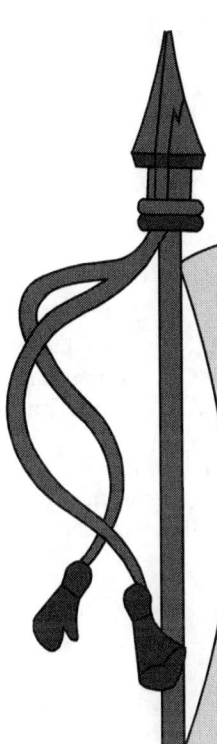

Chapter 11
▶ Hall of Worthies and Other Contributions

Divide the class into small groups and assign each group one of the Korean leaders discussed in the chapter. Have the small groups use the information in the chapter and what they find at the library or on the Internet to collect information about the contributions of the Korean leader they are researching. Groups can then organize the information onto a chart, using illustrations and diagrams to explain the improvements and developments made during the reign of that leader. This project could culminate with a presentation of the charts by each group. Share with the class the assessment rubric at the back of this guide. As each group presents, the rest of the class may want to rate their performance against the rubric.

Chapter 12
▶ A Ming Interview

Divide students into partnerships. Have each pair choose either Ming Taizu or Yongle as their Ming leader to research. Then ask students to use the information in the chapter as well as the information they find in the library or on the Internet to create interview questions for that person. Pairs can then write questions for this leader and the answers they think this person would give, based on the research they did. This project could culminate with students using their word-processing skills to write out the script for the interview. Then students can decide which person will be the Ming leader and which will be the interviewer. They can then present their interviews for the class. Share with the class the assessment rubric at the back of this guide. As each pair presents, the rest of the class may want to rate their performance against the rubric.

TWO TEACHERS: BUDDHA, KONGZI, AND EARLY INDIA AND CHINA PAGES 20–30

FOR HOMEWORK

STUDENT STUDY GUIDE

pages 11–14

CAST OF CHARACTERS

Siddartha Gautama (si-DAHR-thuh Gow-TA-ma) the Buddha ("Enlightened One"), founder of Buddhism

Kong Zhongni (koong joong-nee) or **Kongzi** (KOONG-dzuh) ("Master Kong") Chinese philosopher and teacher known in the West as Confucius

Laozi (laow-dzuh) "Old Master," legendary 6th-century BCE founder of Daoism

Qin Shi Huangdi (chin sher hwong-dee) Unifier and first emperor of China

Mahavira (MA-ha-VEE-ra) founder of Jainism in the 6th–5th centuries BCE

Ashoka (uh-SHOK-uh) Indian king of the Maurya dynasty in India

Emperor Wu Most powerful of the Han rulers; ruled from 140 to 87 BCE

CHAPTER SUMMARY

In the 6th century BCE, two teachers, the Buddha in India and Kongzi in China, developed ways of thought that influenced other parts of Asia. Other important schools included Jainism and Brahmanism (which later evolved into Hinduism) in India, and Daoism and Legalism in China. In the 4th century BCE, the Mauryan state united much of India, and in the 4th century CE the Gupta state reunited much of the same region. In the 3rd century BCE, the Qin and then the Han dynasties unified most of China. Following trade routes, Hinduism and Buddhism spread from India to Southeast and East Asia.

PERFORMANCE OBJECTIVES

▶ To describe the origins, teachings, and influence of Buddhism, Confucianism, Daoism, Legalism, Jainism, and Brahmanism

▶ To identify Qin Shihuangdi and describe his contributions to China

▶ To identify King Ashoka and describe his contributions to India

▶ To analyze the role of the Han dynasty in Chinese history

▶ To explain the importance of trade in spreading religion, particularly Buddhism

BUILDING BACKGROUND

Have students identify as many of the world's religions as they can. Let the class vote to guess the top three or four religions today, in order of the number of adherents. Then compare their guess with the actual ranking: 1) Christianity, 2) Islam, 3) Hinduism, and 4) Buddhism. Tell students that this chapter explains how Buddhism got its start in the 6th century BCE. Add that students will also learn in this chapter about other religions and philosophies that still influence peoples' thoughts, though their followers number far fewer than the previous four: Jainism, Confucianism, Daoism, and Legalism. Add that students will also learn in this chapter about other ways of thought (Jainism, Confucianism, Daoism, and Legalism) that are still influential although they now count fewer followers than the above four religious.

VOCABULARY

exploitation using others for selfish purposes
meditate to think deeply, especially about spiritual matters
radical extreme, fundamental
frugally thriftily
subcontinent a large landmass that is part of a continent
nomadic living in different places
rituals ceremonies

WORKING WITH PRIMARY SOURCES

Read aloud to students the excerpt from the *Lankavatara Sutra* (see page 53 of *The Medieval & Early Modern World Primary Sources and Reference Volume*). Introduce the excerpt by explaining that this sutra, which many Buddhists believe contains the exact words of the Buddha, talks about vegetarianism, an issue that is the subject of much discussion today. Ask: How does being a vegetarian fit in with what you know about Buddhism and what you learn about it in the chapter?

READING COMPREHENSION QUESTIONS

1. What was the Buddha's early life like? (*As a young prince, he had a comfortable and happy life.*)
2. What was Kong Zhongni's new idea about governing? (*Governing should be based not on noble birth but on intelligence, education, and virtue.*)
3. In what ways did Qin Shi Huangdi unite China? (*developing a powerful army, standardizing money and language, building a wall to protect farmers from nomads, building a tomb stocked with clay soldiers, encouraging good farming practices, building canals and irrigation systems*)
4. Why was the branch of Buddhism called Mahayana easier to follow than Theravada? (*Mahayana held that people could become enlightened without leaving family and friends. Theravada required that people must give up everything and become monks to gain enlightenment.*)
5. Were Jainists vegetarians? Why or why not? (*Yes; their most important principle is not to hurt other creatures.*)
6. What is dharma, and how does someone express it? (*Dharma is "truth" or "duty," and one expresses it in Hinduism by being devoted to a god and living a virtuous life according to one's caste.*)
7. What were two important activities of the Han dynasty? (*It used examinations to select public officials and entered into trade on what became known as the Silk Road.*)

CRITICAL THINKING QUESTIONS

1. In what way was Siddartha Gautama extraordinary? (*Possible answer: In response to his distress at seeing people's endless suffering, he meditated and arrived at a new religion, which taught people how to escape from suffering.*)
2. Why do you think no ruler wanted to put Kong Zhongni's ideas about governing into practice? (*Rulers thought that government by virtue was unrealistic and impractical in a world dominated byh warfare among competing states.*)
3. What is one significant difference between Buddhism and Hinduism? (*Possible answer: Buddhists do not believe in a caste system and Hindus do.*)

SOCIAL SCIENCES

Civics Give students photocopies of a Venn diagram (see reproducibles at the back of this guide). Let students use the diagram to compare and contrast the beliefs of Buddhism and Confucianism. Then have students use the diagrams to help them discuss how the life of a devout Buddhist and a devout Confucianist might differ.

THEN and NOW

Buddhism was a new religion of the 6th century BCE that quickly took hold in India and eventually spread throughout Asia. Two much more recent religions are The Church of Jesus Christ of Latter-day Saints (also called the LDS or Mormon Church), and Baha'i. The LDS Church was founded in the United States in 1830 and now has about 12 million adherents worldwide. The Baha'i faith was founded a decade or so later in what is now Iran and has about 6 million followers.

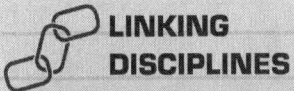

LINKING DISCIPLINES

Art Encourage students to study the portraits of the Buddha and Confucius in this chapter, as well as others they locate. Then have them draw or paint their own portrait of one of these great men.

THE ASIAN WORLD, 600–1500

LITERATURE CONNECTION

Waley, Arthur. *Ballads and Stories from Tun-huang: An Anthology*. London: G. Allen & Unwin, 1960. This compilation includes material from the Tun-huang (Dunhuang) caves in western China. The Tun-huang manuscripts are some of the earliest known works in Buddhism.

Inoue, Yasushi. *Tun-Huang*. Kodansha America, 1983. This novel takes place in 1026, in the remote western frontier of China where a fierce battle is raging. Inoue weaves a story around the Thousand Buddha caves of Tun-huang.

Your students may also be interested in Hermann Hesse's novel *Siddhartha*, which retells the story of the Buddha. Having been translated from the original German, the work is readily available in several editions.

LITERACY TIPS

In addition to using the suggestions in the Supporting Learning and Extending Learning sections, refer back frequently to pages 16–19 for strategies and advice from a literacy coach.

READING AND LANGUAGE ARTS

Reading Nonfiction As students read the chapter, have them write down the name of each religious or philosophical belief as they encounter it in the text. Then they can summarize the most important tenets of the belief. They can copy their notes onto a chart, which can provide them a quick review of many of the most important ideas in the chapter.

Using Language The word *karma* has a specific meaning in Buddhist and Hindu religious beliefs. The word is also used in casual conversation as in the phrase *bad karma*. Have students use a dictionary to compare the formal and informal meanings of *karma*. Ask a volunteer to explain how the informal meaning might have been derived from the formal one.

WRITING

Summary Ask students to sum up the achievements of one of the religious leaders discussed in this chapter. In a short essay, students should give basic biographical information and then describe the person's achievements and the significance of each achievement. the rest of the chapter independently.

SUPPORTING LEARNING

English Language Learners Read aloud the first section of the chapter to students as they follow along in their book. Remind students that proper nouns name specific people, places, and things and that proper nouns are capitalized. Have students point out the proper nouns and identify what they name. Encourage students to pay particular attention to the proper nouns as they read the rest of the chapter independently.

Struggling Readers Have students use the main idea and details graphic organizer (see reproducibles at the back of this guide) to help them understand the tenets of the religions and philosophies discussed in the chapter. Have them use one blackline master for each religion.

EXTENDING LEARNING

Enrichment Let students compare images of the Buddha from various parts of Asia. Encourage students to look for characteristics including pose and physical features that all the images share and ways in which each region's Buddhas are unique.

Extension To each student, assign one of the religions discussed in the chapter. Ask small groups of students, each student representing a different religion, to make a presentation to the rest of the class. Have students describe one aspect of the religion that they liked or one belief that they found especially valuable.

NAME _____ DATE _____

THE EMPIRES OF INDIA

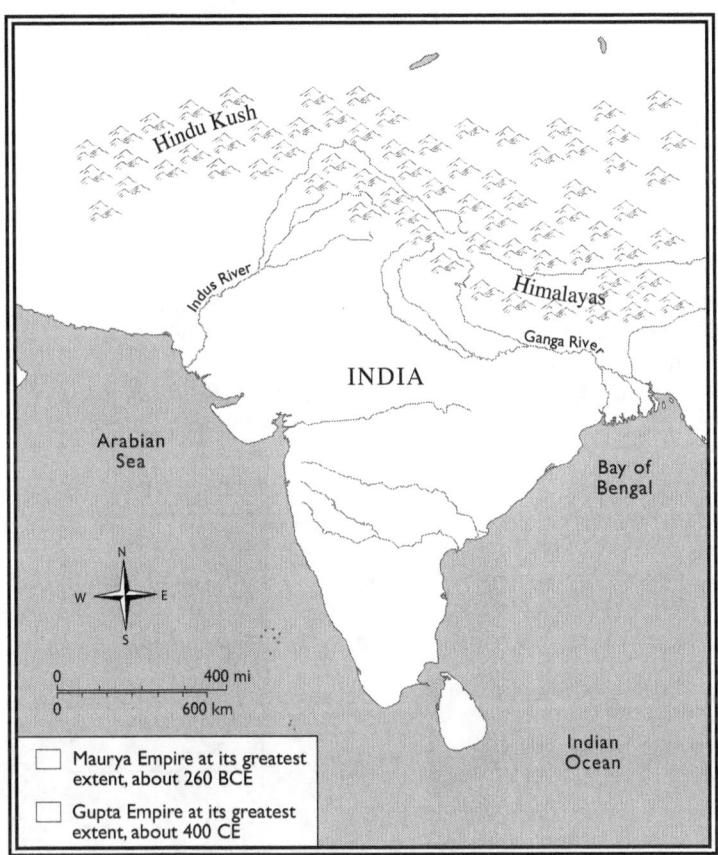

Directions

Make the following changes to show the locations and extents of the Maurya and Gupta Empires in India.

1. Use a pattern or shading to indicate the Maurya Empire at its greatest extent (about 260 BCE).

2. Use a pattern or shading to indicate the Gupta Empire at its greatest extent (about 400 CE). Key both patterns in the legend.

3. Use a colored pencil to show the trade routes in and out of India that led to the spreading of Buddhism and Hinduism to Southeast Asia.

4. In a different color, trace the trade routes from India to the kingdoms in Central Asia.

5. On both trade routes, what goods from India were traded in these other areas?

_____

_____

CHAPTER 1 BLM   THE ASIAN WORLD, 600–1500   **29**

PRIMARY SOURCES

Directions

Read the quotations. Then answer the questions.

> The noble-minded person loves virtue; the ordinary-minded person loves what serves his own interests
> —Kong Zhongni

> Ancients and moderns have different customs; the present and the past follow different courses of action. To attempt to apply a benevolent and lenient government to the people in a desperate age is about the same as trying to drive wild horses without reins.
> — Hanfeizi, Legalist philosopher, from *The Book of Hanfeizi,* about 240 BCE

> Benevolence is difficult; he who performs a benevolent act accomplishes something difficult. I have performed much that is benevolent. Benevolence shall also be practiced by my sons, my grandsons and their descendants, even until the very dissolution of the universe.
> —King Ashoka, Indian ruler, inscription on a stone table, about 240 BCE

1. What Confucian belief did the first quotation express?

2. Contrast the second and third quotations. How do the writers' ideas differ?

3. What did Hanfeizi mean when he compared governing to driving horses?

4. Which quotation do you think is the most significant for people today? Why?

CHAPTER TEST 1

THE ASIAN WORLD, 600–1500

NAME _____ DATE _____

A. MULTIPLE CHOICE

Circle the letter of the best answer to each question.

1. How did Siddartha become the Buddha?
   a. He became a king.
   b. He saw the people's poverty, exploitation, and illness.
   c. He meditated under a holy tree.
   d. He studied at a famous university.

2. According to the Buddha, what is the source of suffering?
   a. evil
   b. desire
   c. ignorance
   d. poverty

3. What was Kong Zhongni's radical new idea about government service?
   a. Government jobs should be inherited.
   b. Government jobs should go to nobles.
   c. Government jobs should be based on ability.
   d. Government jobs should result from elections.

4. In Mahayana Buddhism, what sacrifice does a Bodhisattva make?
   a. takes a vow of poverty
   b. leaves one's family to wander the countryside
   c. studies one's entire lifetime
   d. postpones enlightenment to save others

5. What was an accomplishment of Han Wudi?
   a. expanding the frontiers
   b. advocating Buddhism
   c. suppressing Confucianism
   d. living frugally

B. SHORT ANWER

Answer these questions in two or three sentences.

6. What were some of the major accomplishments of Qin Shi Huangdi?

   _____
   _____
   _____

7. Explain the significance of trade to the growth of Buddhism and Hinduism in Asia.

   _____
   _____
   _____

C. ESSAY

In an essay on a separate piece of paper, summarize the core beliefs of Buddhism. Describe where it spread and why.

THE ASIAN WORLD, 600–1500   CHAPTER 1 TEST   **31**

CHINA UNITED, AGAIN: THE SUI AND TANG DYNASTIES
PAGES 31–42

STUDENT STUDY GUIDE
pages 15–18

CAST OF CHARACTERS

Sui Wendi (sway one-dee) personal name Yang Jian, Chinese emperor and founder of the Sui dynasty

Li Yuan (lee yooann) founder and first emperor of China's Tang dynasty

Tang Taizong (tahng tie-dzoong), personal name Li Shimin (lee sher-min) second emperor of China's Tang dynasty

Xuanzang (syuan-dzahng) Chinese Buddhist pilgrim to India

Wu Zhao (woo jao) imperial concubine who became China's only female emperor

Tang Xuanzong (tahng syuan-dzoong) Chinese emperor during Tang dynasty who had a disastrous affair with concubine Yang Guifei

Wang Wei (wong way) Chinese Buddhist poet and painter

Li Bai (lee buy) Chinese Tang dynasty poet

Du Fu (doo foo) Chinese Tang dynasty poet

CHAPTER SUMMARY

Yang Jian of the Sui dynasty reunited China in 589 for the first time since 220. The Sui dynasty was unable to hold on to power for long. Li Yuan led a rebellion and proclaimed the Tang dynasty in 618. His son Li Shimin, one of China's most admired emperors, enacted educational, tax, and land reforms. Chinese Buddhists encouraged the discovery of printing and popularized tea drinking. Poetry flourished. Tang emperors expanded the empire and one, Wu Zhao, became the only female emperor in Chinese history. The Tang dynasty gradually weakened and finally fell in 907.

PERFORMANCE OBJECTIVES

- To identify Sui dynasty emperors
- To describe events and achievements of the Sui dynasty
- To identify Tang dynasty emperors
- To describe events and achievements of the Tang dynasty
- To analyze Chinese Buddhism and its influences

BUILDING BACKGROUND

Have students debate the personal qualities and abilities that make a president great. Encourage them to name their favorite American president and explain why, in their opinion, he was the best. Point out that the qualities that make great leaders vary depending on the place and the time. Ask students to read the chapter to find out what qualities a person would need to become a great emperor of the Sui or Tang dynasty.

VOCABULARY

regent person who acts for a ruler
imperial relating to an emperor
campaign series of military operations
famine drastic food shortage
conspiracy agreement between two or more people to commit a crime
stroke loss of brain function caused by blockage of blood flowing to the brain
regime government in power

WORKING WITH PRIMARY SOURCES

Ask a volunteer to read aloud to the class the excerpt from *The Life of Xuanzang* (see page 54 of *The Medieval & Early Modern World Primary Sources and Reference Volume*). Emphasize Xuanzang's importance to the spread of Buddhism in China. Explain that though Xuanzang was a real person, stories of his 15-year journey became exaggerated and eventually took on mythical qualities.

GEOGRAPHY CONNECTION

Measurement China's vast size made it particularly challenging for one leader to unify and rule effectively. Review the map on pages 14–15 of the Student Edition, and work with the class to calculate some of the distances between major Chinese cities using the mileage scale. China's sheer size and limited access to coastal trade routes also made inland transportation essential. Discuss with the class the importance of the Grand Canal, built by Su Wendi and his son Yangdi in the late 6th and early 7th centuries, and explain how this helped link the rice-producing regions in the south with the north.

READING COMPREHENSION QUESTIONS

1. What was Yang Jian's biggest achievement? (*reuniting China*)
2. In what way was the Sui dynasty like the Qin dynasty 800 years earlier? (*Both unified China, but neither was able to hold onto power for long.*)
3. Why were the people discontented under the Sui rulers? (*They were required to put into much time working on projects and fighting in the army.*)
4. What circumstance finally caused Li Yuan and Li Shimin to rebel? (*They were already facing conspiracy charges, so they had nothing to lose.*)
5. Why was Li Shimin one of China's greatest emperors? (*He listened to criticism from his advisors; by selecting more officials through written exams, he improved education and participation in the arts; he reformed taxes and land distribution; he created more jobs for merchants and craftspeople.*)
6. What belief did the Pure Land school of Buddhism follow? (*It encouraged personal devotion to the Bodhisattva of Infinite Mercy.*)
7. How did Buddhism encourage the invention of printing? (*Buddhists wished to win followers by supplying them with texts (sutras), but copying them by hand took too long, so they had the idea of carving the texts into wooden blocks and using them to print copies of the sutras.*)
8. What was most unusual about Tang ruler Wu Zhao? (*She was a woman.*)

CRITICAL THINKING QUESTIONS

1. Choose three adjectives that describe Wu Zhao most accurately. Why did you choose each one? (*Possible answer: Ambitious because she was determined to rule, ruthless because she had the emperor's number one wife killed, capable because she ruled China well for 15 years.*)
2. Why do you suppose Chinese dynasties such as the Sui and Tang were unable to keep China united? (*Possible answer: China was too big and diverse to hold together forever; in addition, dynasties begin to become corrupt after a while.*)
3. How did the invention of printing affect learning in China? (*Possible answer: It made it easier for not only Buddhist sutras but other kinds of texts to spread more easily among Chinese who could read.*)

SOCIAL SCIENCES

Science, Technology, and Society Distribute to students copies of the main idea map (see reproducibles at the back of this guide). Let students use the map to explore the invention of printing in China. Have them write *Invention of Printing* in the center oval. Then encourage students to reread the information in their text and do further research on the topic. They can sum up what they learn in the detail ovals of the map. Let students add as many detail ovals or use as many masters as necessary.

THEN and NOW

Poetry flourished in China during the Tang dynasty. Many centuries later, people still enjoy the poems of leading Tang-era poets Wang Wei, Li Bai, Du Fu, and others. Here is a poem by Wang Wei, "On Parting with Spring."

Day after day we can't help growing older.

Year after year spring can't help seeming younger.

Come let's enjoy our winecup today,

Not pity the flowers fallen!

Do you think the poet's message still makes sense?

LINKING DISCIPLINES

Literature Ask students to locate poems of Wang Wei, Li Bai, and Du Fu. After they read several examples of each poet's work, have them choose a poem to read aloud to their classmates. Encourage students to memorize the poem and recite it dramatically and meaningfully.

THE ASIAN WORLD, 600–1500

LITERATURE CONNECTION

Li Bai is considered to be the foremost poet of the Tang dynasty. The website Poem Hunter includes the text of many of his poems in translation, including "A Song of Happiness": www.poemhunter.com/li-bai/poet-20138/. China Online also includes information on Li Bai, as well as links to his poetry in translation: http://chineseculture.about.com/library/weekly/aa071001a.htm.

READING AND LANGUAGE ARTS

Reading Nonfiction   Have students use the sequence of events graphic organizer (see reproducibles at the back of this guide) to help them remember the order of the rulers in the Sui and Tang dynasties. Have them write the name of each ruler, the dates of his or her rule, and the name of the dynasty in each box.

Using Language   Alert students that they will notice quite a few proper adjectives in this chapter. Remind students that a proper adjective such as Chinese describes a particular person, place, or thing. Add that proper adjectives are always capitalized. Have students find other examples of proper adjectives in the chapter.

WRITING

Descriptive Paragraph   Ask students to choose one of the emperors they read about in the chapter. Have them write a one-paragraph sketch of the ruler's personality and accomplishments.

SUPPORTING LEARNING

English Language Learners   Ask small groups or pairs of students to read the chapter together. After students read each page silently, have them discuss it, figuring out or looking up unknown words and summarizing important ideas. Encourage them to mark puzzling passages and ask you, an aide, or a student whose first language is English what they mean.

Struggling Readers   To introduce the topic of the chapter, have a volunteer read aloud the title. Call on students to explain what the words *united* and *dynasties* mean. Then read aloud the first two paragraphs and discuss them with students. Have students read the rest of the chapter independently. Encourage them to take notes on important ideas.

EXTENDING LEARNING

Enrichment   Challenge students to find out what life was like for commoners during the Sui and Tang dynasties. For example, the text mentions that common people were accustomed to doing unpaid labor on public works projects for several weeks a year. What else did their emperors require of them? What did they do when they weren't working for the emperor? How hard were their lives?

Extension   Let pairs of students work together to improvise conversations between one of the famous people in the chapter and an interviewer. After they decide on the subject of the interview, students should reread the information about him or her. The person playing the part of the historical figure should try to stay in character, and the interviewer should ask relevant and intriguing questions. Tape the interviews if possible so that students can share them with friends and family.

LITERACY TIPS

In addition to using the suggestions in the Supporting Learning and Extending Learning sections, refer back frequently to pages 16–19 for strategies and advice from a literacy coach.

NAME   **DATE**

PRIMARY SOURCES

THE DEATH OF A CONCUBINE

Directions

Read the passage from "Song of Unending Sorrow" by Bai Juyi (about 820). Then answer the questions.

> From the ninefold palace wall rose plumes of dust and smoke.
> A thousand wagons, ten thousand horsemen, travelled southwestwards
> With the royal banners waving. But then they halted,
> West of the capital, not more than a hundred miles.
> The six-division army would go no further, no matter the danger,
> Until he gave up his moth-browed beauty to die, trampled by horses.
> Her gold-flowered hair combs fell to the ground, her kingfisher-feather crown,
> Her trembling bird-ornaments of gold, her jade hairpins;
> The Son of Heaven could only cover his eyes, unable to help her,
> As blood and tears flowed together.
> Dust swirled in yellow clouds, the wind blew cold,
> As the exile-road wound upwards over Sword Watchtower Pass.

1. What does this part of the poem describe?

_____
_____
_____
_____

2. Sometimes details can make the description of a disaster especially moving. Which details did poet Bai Juyi include that you find touching?

_____
_____
_____
_____

3. What do you think of the decision Emperor Xuanzong made that was described in this passage? Give reasons for your answer.

_____
_____
_____
_____

PRIMARY SOURCES

Directions

Read the quotations. Then answer the questions.

> Now Buddha was a man of the barbarians who did not speak the language of China and wore clothes of a different fashion. His sayings did not concern the ways of our ancient kings.
> —Tang Confucian intellectual Han Yu, "Memorial on the Bone of the Buddha," about 820

> We monks, having in mind merely our longing for the Buddhist teachings, have come from afar to this benevolent land with our hearts set on sacred places and our spirits rejoicing in the pilgrimage.
> —Ennin, Japanese Buddhist monk visiting China, in his diary, 840

1. How would you describe the difference in tone between the first and second quotations?

2. What does the first quotation tell the reader about Confucianism?

3. What does the first quotation indicate about how the Chinese viewed foreigners?

4. Why might the views of the writer of the second quotation not be a typical?

CHAPTER TEST 2

THE ASIAN WORLD, 600–1500

NAME _____ DATE _____

A. MULTIPLE CHOICE

Circle the letter of the best answer to each question.

1. What important event happened in 589?
   a. Yang Jian was born to a powerful and wealthy family.
   b. Yang Jian defeated the Chens and united China.
   c. Yang Jian appointed himself prime minister.
   d. The Duke of Sui died before appointing an heir.

2. Which of the following did **not** influence Yang Jian?
   a. Confucianism
   b. Daoism
   c. Brahmanism
   d. Buddhism

3. What led up to the beginning of Tang Taizong's reign?
   a. He overthrew the Sui dynasty.
   b. He had the crown prince killed.
   c. He passed a merit examination.
   d. His father died suddenly.

4. Which was a characteristic of Confucian education?
   a. conducting scientific experiments
   b. learning foreign languages
   c. participating in the arts
   d. giving speeches

5. What was an important reason that Chinese Buddhist monks were interested in drinking tea?
   a. Tea kept them alert during religious ceremonies.
   b. Tea was the most delicious beverage they had ever tasted.
   c. The Buddha had been a tea drinker.
   d. Tea kept them from feeling hunger pangs.

6. How did Emperor Gaozong's stroke benefit Wu Zhao?
   a. She became empress.
   b. She was promoted to first wife.
   c. She was appointed a public official.
   d. She ran the government for him.

B. SHORT ANSWER

Answer each question in two or three sentences.

7. What where the major accomplishments of the Sui dynasty?
   _____
   _____

8. What were the problems of the Tang dynasty after the 830s?
   _____
   _____

C. ESSAY

In an essay on a separate piece of paper, describe the strengthening of China's unity under Tang Taizong.

RAJAS AND SULTANS: THE STRUGGLE FOR INDIA, PAGES 43–54

STUDENT STUDY GUIDE

pages 19–22

CAST OF CHARACTERS

Mahadeviyakka (MA-ha-DEV-ee-YAK-ka) Indian woman religious poet

Harsha Vardhana (HAR-sha var-DAHN-ha) north Indian conqueror.

Muhammad (mu-HAM-mahd) prophet, founder of Islam

Muhammad ibn Qasim (mu-HAM-mahd ib-in KASS-im) Arab prince, conquered Indian province of Sind

Mahmud of Gazni (ma-MOOD of GAHZ-nee) Muslim ruler of Afghanistan, invaded India

Bhoj (BOE-ja) philosopher-king of Paramara, India

Muhammad Ghori (mu-HAM-mahd GORE-ee) Persian ruler who conquered northern India

Qutb-ud-Ddn Aybak (KUTB-ood-deen AYE-bahk) first sultan of Dehli, India

CHAPTER SUMMARY

India was difficult to unify because of its geographic, economic, ethnic, and religious diversity. Harsha Vardhana succeeded in controlling most of northern India, but his empire collapsed after he died in 647. Arab prince Muhammad ibn Qasim conquered cities of Sind (in present-day Pakistan), exposing Indians to Islam and the Islamic world to simplified numbers and the concept of zero. For 500 years, from the early 8th to the early 13th century, Northern India endured wars, conquests, and uprisings. Much of India came to be ruled by Muslims whose ancestors had come from other places, while most common people remained Hindus.

PERFORMANCE OBJECTIVES

▶ To describe the geographic, economic, ethnic, and religious diversity of India
▶ To compare various regions of India
▶ To analyze the impact of Islam on India
▶ To summarize the reigns of various rulers of regions of India

BUILDING BACKGROUND

Let students page through the chapter, studying the illustrations and reading the title, headings, and captions. Ask students to predict the overall topic of the chapter and the subtopics the chapter will include. Have students jot down their predictions in their history journal. After they finish reading the chapter, encourage them to check the accuracy of their predictions.

VOCABULARY

diverse made up of distinct characteristics
salvation asving from death or punishment after death
tolerant inclined to respect or at least permit the beliefs and practices of others
access getting into
realm territory
benefactors people who give aid or do good to others
clarity clearness of thought

WORKING WITH PRIMARY SOURCES

After you read aloud or summarize the introduction on page 61 of *The Medieval & Early Modern World Primary Sources and Reference Volume* for the class, ask a volunteer to read aloud the selection, "Whistle While You Work," from a song by South Asian poet Ratanabi. Remind students that the Ganga, or Ganges, is a sacred river to Hindus. After taking time to let students respond freely to the text, ask them to describe its tone.

GEOGRAPHY CONNECTION

Movement Have students study the map on page 48 of the Student Edition. Explain that it uses shading to show how the influence of Islam spread east, through Central Asia and into India. Review the names of the regions where Islam spread: Persia, Afghanistan, Panjab, Sind, and so forth. Identify major rivers labeled on the map, plus the Tigris and Euphrates Rivers, leading to the Persian Gulf. Discuss with the class the significance of the Arab conquest of Sind (India was now a neighbor to an Islamic region). Ask students to explain why Islam spread east from Arabia by way of Persia, rather than spreading directly east across the Arabian Peninsula (*Because the Arabian Peninsula was an impassable desert, so trading routes from Mecca went north through the Near East, following the Tigris and Euphrates to the Persian Gulf.*)

READING COMPREHENSION QUESTIONS

1. What word best describes the geography of India? (*Possible answers: varied, diverse*)
2. Which new religion arrived in India during the early 8th century? (*Islam*)
3. What were two reasons Muslims felt obliged to try to conquer parts of India? (*to spread their religion; to acquire some of the wealth of India*)
4. Why did Muslims respect such religions as Judaism and Christianity, but were less respectful of Buddhism and Hinduism? (*Judaism and Christianity believe in one god, the same god as Islam, but Hinduism and Buddhism believe in many gods or in a single god different from that of Judaism, Christianity and Islam.*)
5. What was Nalanda University, where was it located, and what lasting effect did it have? (*Nalanda University was the world's oldest Buddhist university; it was located in northeast India in the state of Pala; monks from the university introduced Buddhism to Tibet and to much of the rest of East and Southeast Asia.*)
6. What attracted some Hindus to Islam? (*its simple, clear message of submission to God and emphasis on justice and equality*)
7. What adjective would you use to describe India during the period from the early 8th to the early 13th century? (*Possible answers: chaotic, confusing, violent, unsettled; also diverse, culturally rich, interesting*)

CRITICAL THINKING QUESTIONS

1. Why do you think the simplified numerals that actually came from India are known in the West as Arabic numerals? (*Possible answer: The Arabs introduced the knowledge of this way of writing numbers throughout the world.*)
2. Why did Muslims and Hindus have different opinions about Mahmud of Gazni who led an army that raided Panjab? (*Possible answer: Muslims approved of him because he was spreading Islam, but Hindus hated and feared him because he killed many Hindus and destroyed many of their temples.*)
3. Why do you think that most common people of India kept their Hindu faith rather than converting to Islam? (*Islam was regarded as a foreign religion by some. Its use of force repelled many people.*)

SOCIAL SCIENCES

Economics Distribute the T-chart graphic organizer (see reproducibles at the back of this guide). Let students use the chart to list the economic effects of the Arab's adoption of the Indian numeric system and the concept of zero. Ask: What effect might these discoveries have had on business practices, on accounting, and on trade?

THEN and NOW

Artists have depicted the Hindu trinity of gods—Brahma the creator of the universe, Vishnu the preserver, and Shiva the destroyer—since the beginnings of Hinduism some 1500 years BCE. Today Hindus and non-Hindus alike can view sculptures of these gods in art museums around the world. Students can see examples of Hindu sculpture on the websites of such museums as the Metropolitan Museum of Art in New York City.

LINKING DISCIPLINES

Science Have students research the two mathematical concepts that the Arabs took from India: what people today call Arabic numerals and the concept of zero. Ask students to discuss the impact of each of these ideas.

THE ASIAN WORLD, 600–1500

READING AND LANGUAGE ARTS

Reading Nonfiction Guide students to use the images shown throughout the chapter (maps as well as photographs) to create a visual summary of the information discussed. Students may photocopy or redraw the visuals and then write a caption that summarizes the content represented by each image.

Using Language Help students appreciate the power of precise language to create vivid images. Ask students to reread the song by Mahadeviyakka on page 43. Point to the words *sapphires* and *jasmine-white*, and ask what effect the poet would have created by using the less-exact words *gems* and *white flowers* in their place. Ask students to close their eyes and try to picture a gem or a white flower. Urge students to use exact words in their writing to create vivid images in readers' minds.

WRITING

Celebrity Interview Let students work in pairs. Ask one student to take the part of an interviewer and the other to play one of the prominent people discussed in this chapter. Encourage the interviewer to ask questions about the person's early years, achievements, and goals for the future. Ask the student playing the celebrity to use the information in the chapter along with imagination to answer the interviewer's questions.

SUPPORTING LEARNING

English Language Learners On the board list idiomatic expressions from the chapter. Some of these include the following: *paying no attention, have nothing to do with him, ways of life, wholehearted support,* and *paving the way*. Explain what the expressions mean as you write their definitions on the board. Then ask volunteers to use the expressions in sentences. Keep the list on the board so students can consult it as they read the chapter.

Struggling Readers Go over the names of the people in the chapter with students. Write each name from the Cast of Characters, along with its pronunciation. Pronounce each name several times, first alone and then with the students saying it along with you. Make sure students are familiar with each name and its pronunciation so that these difficult names do not intimidate them when they encounter the names in the text.

EXTENDING LEARNING

Enrichment Let students explore a topic that was briefly mentioned in the chapter such as the poetry of Mahadeviyakka, Tantric Buddhism, or the worship of Shiva. Encourage them to share what they learned in informal presentations to their classmates.

Extension Let volunteers take on the persona of one of the people discussed in this chapter. In speeches to the class, have them introduce themselves and explain the reasons for the actions they took in their lifetimes.

LITERACY TIPS

In addition to using the suggestions in the Supporting Learning and Extending Learning sections, refer back frequently to pages 16–19 for strategies and advice from a literacy coach.

NAME   **DATE**

HARSHA'S DYNASTY IN INDIA, 640

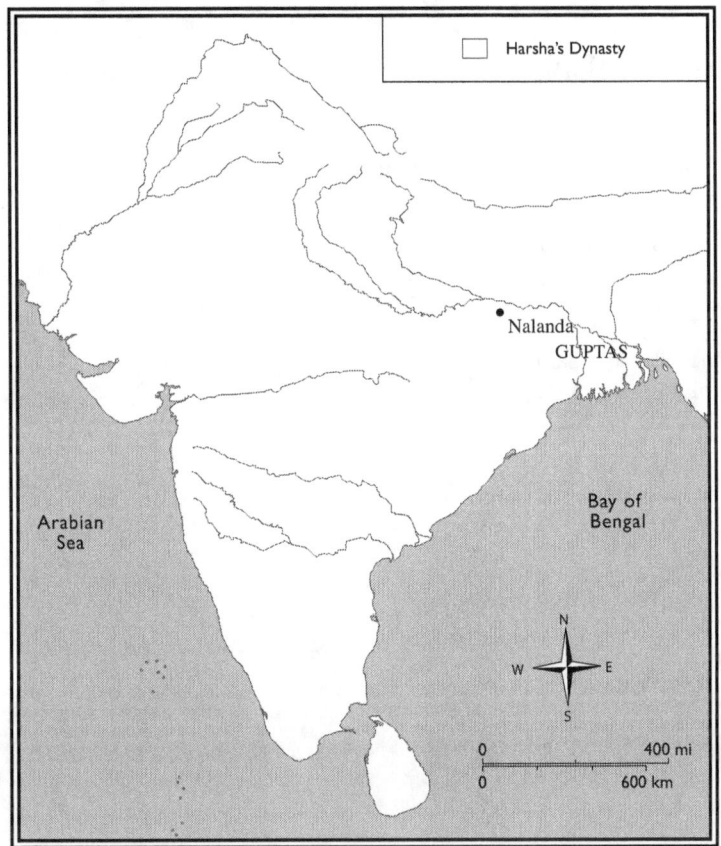

Directions

Make the following changes to the map to show the range of Harsha's conquests of northern India about 640. Then answer the questions.

1. Use shading or a pattern to show the extent of Harsha's land. Key this pattern to the legend.

2. Label the following rivers: Indus River, Bramaputra River, Ganga River, and Jamuna River

3. Label the following areas: KASHMIR, PANJAB, NEPAL, GUJARAT, INDIA

4. How long did Harsha's empire last, and why did it end?

_____
_____
_____

5. Trace the direction of Harsha's conquests, beginning with his place of birth.

PRIMARY SOURCES

THE WAR GOD BATTLES A DEMON

Directions

Read the excerpt from "The Birth of the War God" by Kalidasa. Then answer the questions.

> A fearful flock of evil birds,
> Ready for the joy of eating the army of demons [Taraka's army]
> Flew over the host of the gods,
> And clouded the sun.
>
> A wind continually fluttered their umbrellas and banners,
> And troubled their eyes with clouds of whirling dust,
> So that the trembling horses and elephants
> And the great chariots could not be seen.
>
> Suddenly monstrous serpents, as black as powdered soot,
> Scattering poison from their upraised heads,
> Frightful in form,
> Appeared in the army's path.
>
> The sun put on a ghastly robe
> Of great and terrible snakes, curling together
> As if to mark his joy
> At the death of the terrible demon.
>
> And before the very disc of the sun
> Jackals bayed harshly together,
> As though eager fiercely to lap the blood
> Of the king of the foes of the gods, fallen in battle. . . .
>
> The host of the foe was jostled together.
> The great elephants stumbled, the horses fell,
> And all the foot soldiers clung together in fear,
> As the earth trembled and the ocean rose to shake the mountains.

1. How well do you think these verses capture the feeling of warfare? Support your answer with details from the poem.
_____
_____

2. Who has won this battle? Who has lost?
_____
_____

3. The poem is filled with vivid images. What are some of your favorites?
_____
_____

CHAPTER TEST 3

THE ASIAN WORLD, 600–1500

NAME _____ **DATE** _____

A. MULTIPLE CHOICE

Circle the letter of the best answer to each question.

1. What is a crop of the wet lowlands of India?
   a. millet
   b. rice
   c. coconuts
   d. wheat

2. Over which part of India did King Harsha have control?
   a. north
   b. south
   c. east
   d. west

3. What does the word *Islam* mean?
   a. salvation
   b. belief
   c. submission
   d. authentic

4. Which region of India was particularly noted for its beautiful temples and sculpture?
   a. Sind
   b. Chola
   c. Pala
   d. Panjab

5. Which region of India was conquered twice by Muslims a century and a half apart?
   a. Sind
   b. Chola
   c. Pala
   d. Panjab

B. SHORT ANSWER

Answer these questions in two or three sentences.

6. Explain why mathematics was called "the Indian art" in Arabic.

   _____
   _____
   _____
   _____

7. Why were Muslims more respectful of Christianity and Judaism than they were of Buddhism and Hinduism?

   _____
   _____
   _____
   _____

C. ESSAY

On a separate piece of paper, summarize the impact of the Islamic presence in India. Use facts from the chapter to support your statements.

CHAPTER 4

TRADE IF BY LAND AND TRADE IF BY SEA: MERCHANTS, RELIGION, AND IDEAS PAGES 55–65

FOR HOMEWORK
STUDENT STUDY GUIDE
pages 23–26

CAST OF CHARACTERS

Ibn Sina (IB-en SEE-nah) Islamic scientist and scholar, known in medieval Europe as Avicenna

Airlangga (EYE-er-LANG-ga) Hindu king of an island state in Southeast Asia

CHAPTER SUMMARY

Beginning in the 2nd century BCE, the Silk Road, a network of paths that connected China, India, and the Middle East, was a vital trade route for objects, ideas, and information. For example, the Chinese exported paper, silk, and paper-making technology. A network of maritime shipping routes connected the Mediterranean area, India, China, and Southeast Asia. When one means of transportation became too dangerous, traders used the other. By the end of the 15th century, trade began to be taken over by Europeans, and the cultural ties between India and Southeast Asia weakened.

PERFORMANCE OBJECTIVES

- To define the term *Silk Road*
- To describe Silk Road trade routes and the goods, ideas, and information they carried
- To analyze the effect of the Silk Road on religion and culture
- To describe how ocean trade was conducted
- To identify the maritime trade network and describe the goods it transported
- To analyze the effects of maritime trade on the region

BUILDING BACKGROUND

Initiate a discussion with the class about today's international trade. Ask students to identify which nations trade with each other, by what means that trade is conducted, and the time needed to transport goods, services, and technology. Help students realize that contemporary trade is global, ideas travel nearly instantaneously, and material goods are transported rapidly every day by air, train, truck, and rail, as well as by ships. Ask students to fill out a Venn diagram (see reproducibles at the back of this guide) to compare trade today with trade in Asia before the 15th century.

VOCABULARY

caravan a group of travelers journeying together
supple easily bent, pliable
aromatic fragrant
maritime relating to the sea
dominated controlled
verdant green with growth

44 CHAPTER 4

WORKING WITH PRIMARY SOURCES

Tell the class that one technology the Chinese exported along the Silk Road was papermaking, which Muslims used to produce copies of the Quran, the Islamic holy book. Read aloud the quotations on page 58 from *Book of Curious and Entertaining Information*, as well as the words of Ibn Sina about the royal library of Bukhara. Ask students to discuss the importance of papermaking technology to the spread of knowledge. Have them compare the invention of paper with the invention of the computer in terms of dissemination of information.

READING COMPREHENSION QUESTIONS

1. What was the Silk Road? (*a network of paths from China connecting oases and towns; some routes leading to Persia, some to India, and some toward the Middle East and Mediterranean*)

2. Travel along the Silk Road could be dangerous, so why did people do it? (*The Silk Road was the main connection between east and west Eurasia, so people traveled it to make money from trade and seek solace in religion.*)

3. What was "down-the-line" trade? (*a process by which goods traveled through several middlemen on their way to their ultimate destination so that goods traveled much farther than traders did*)

4. Why was papermaking so important to Muslims? (*They needed a cheap, durable writing material to reproduce copies of the Quran needed to spread their faith.*)

5. How do we know that religious ideas traveled the Silk Road? (*People built places of worship, made religious artwork, and left tablets and other religious records.*)

6. Why did Chinese maritime trade increase beginning in the 12th century? (*Shipbuilding technology improved and so did navigational instruments, especially the magnetic compass.*)

7. What did Chinese merchants export to the tropical south, and what did they receive in return? (*They exported silk and porcelain in return for spices, sandalwood, rhinoceros horn, sea slugs, pearls, and precious stones.*)

8. How did the monsoon winds affect trade in the Indian Ocean? (*Ships from Arabia used the late summer monsoons to sail to India. The ships would return home when the monsoon winds changed direction. The monsoon also permitted seasonal trade in the Indian Ocean and South China Sea.*)

CRITICAL THINKING QUESTIONS

1. What effect does trade have on ideas, beliefs, and culture? Use examples from the chapter in your answer. (*Possible answer: Trade increases the flow of ideas among peoples, enriching them by exposing them to new beliefs and technologies. For example, Muslims used Chinese papermaking techniques to print the Quran on paper, extending their beliefs to the many more people. Non-Buddhists were exposed to Buddhist beliefs from Buddhist temples, sculptures, and wall paintings that they saw along the Silk Road.*)

2. What was the relationship between the cost of goods and the distance they traveled? Why? (*The farther goods traveled, the greater the number of merchants who handled them, each of whom had to make a profit by increasing the price.*)

3. Why did cultural ties between India and Southeast Asia weaken after most maritime trade was gradually taken over by Europeans? (*The Indians and the people of Southeast Asia saw and talked to each other less frequently, so the cultural ties weakened.*)

THEN and NOW

Camels have helped people live in and travel through deserts for many centuries. Even today, when people can buy motorized vehicles adapted to desert conditions, they often choose to use camels. Camels often cost less, require less "fuel," are less likely to break down, and can provide a source of food and drink in emergencies.

LINKING DISCIPLINES

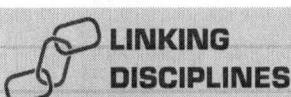

Science Have students do research to find out how silk is produced, starting with silkworms and ending with silk fabric. Ask them to show what they learned in a poster of the steps in making silk. Encourage classroom experts on the silk making process to answer their classmates' questions about the process.

THE ASIAN WORLD, 600–1500

LITERATURE CONNECTION

Wriggins, Sally Hovey. *Xuanzang: A Buddhist Pilgrim on the Silk Road.* Westview Press, 1998. Tells the story of a young monk named Xuanzang, who left China in 639 on the Silk Road to make a remarkable and unprecedented pilgrimage to India.

Many collections of Chinese Literature in translation, many heavily influenced by the Tang dynasty, are available. Among these are:

Birch, Cyril. *Anthology of Chinese Literature.* New York: Grove Press; 1965, 1972. In two volumes: *From Early Times to the 14th Century* (volume 1); *From the 14th Century to the Present Day* (volume 2).

Mair, Victor H. *The Shorter Columbia Anthology of Traditional Chinese Literature.* New York: Columbia University Press, 2000.

LITERACY TIPS

In addition to using the suggestions in the Supporting Learning and Extending Learning sections, refer back frequently to pages 16–19 for strategies and advice from a literacy coach.

SOCIAL SCIENCES

Science, Technology, and Society Let students discuss the impact of technologies related to paper and silk making, as well as improvements in maritime technologies, such as the magnetic compass. Ask: How did the cultures that invented these technologies benefit? How did trading partners benefit?

READING AND LANGUAGE ARTS

Reading Nonfiction Ask students to use the T-chart (see reproducibles at the back of this guide) as they read the chapter to help them analyze the causes and effects of land- and sea-based trade. Work as a class to begin the chart. Have a volunteer read the third paragraph of the chapter aloud. Ask: What does the paragraph say caused people to travel the Silk Road? (*the lure of profit and adventure*) What were two possible dangers of travel on the Silk Road? (*attack by bandits, death from thirst or starvation*) Let students write these causes and effects on their chart and continue looking for causes and effects independently.

Using Language Write the word *monsoon* on the board and have a volunteer define it. If necessary, remind students that a monsoon is a wind system that reverses direction seasonally. Tell students that *monsoon* has an interesting word history. It originally came from an Arabic word *mawsim*, "season," through the Portuguese *monção* and Dutch *monssoen*. Let students speculate about why the word traveled and how it did so.

WRITING

Persuasive Essay Have students imagine that they are a trader in Asia during the time discussed in this chapter. Have them choose whether they would prefer to travel on the Silk Road or by sea. Let them write a short persuasive essay trying to convince possible fellow travelers that the mode of travel they prefer is better than the alternative.

SUPPORTING LEARNING

English Language Learners Have a volunteer read the title aloud. To help students understand the topic and main ideas of the chapter, define the words *networks*, *commerce*, and *culture* in simple language. Then read and discuss the headings and first paragraphs that follow them.

Struggling Readers Let students preview the chapter to predict the sorts of information it will include. Ask students to read the title, headings, captions, and first and last paragraphs. Then have them share predictions about the contents of the chapter. Ask students to write several predictions in their history journals and see how accurate those predictions were as they read the chapter.

EXTENDING LEARNING

Enrichment Let students research an aspect of trade in Asia before the 15th century that interests them, for example, travel by camel, how paper or silk was made, or unusual items such as rhinoceros horn or peacocks, that were traded in Asia. You may wish to have students who are interested in the same topics work together. Ask students to present short oral reports to share interesting facts and anecdotes about their topic with their classmates.

Extension Have small groups of students use paper, books, pens, or other objects to demonstrate how "down-the-line" trade operated on the Silk Road. Ask students to "buy" and "sell" an item as it passes through several of their hands with its value increasing each time it is bought and sold.

CHAPTER BLM 4

THE ASIAN WORLD, 600–1500

NAME   **DATE**

Directions
Use the map to answer the questions that follow.

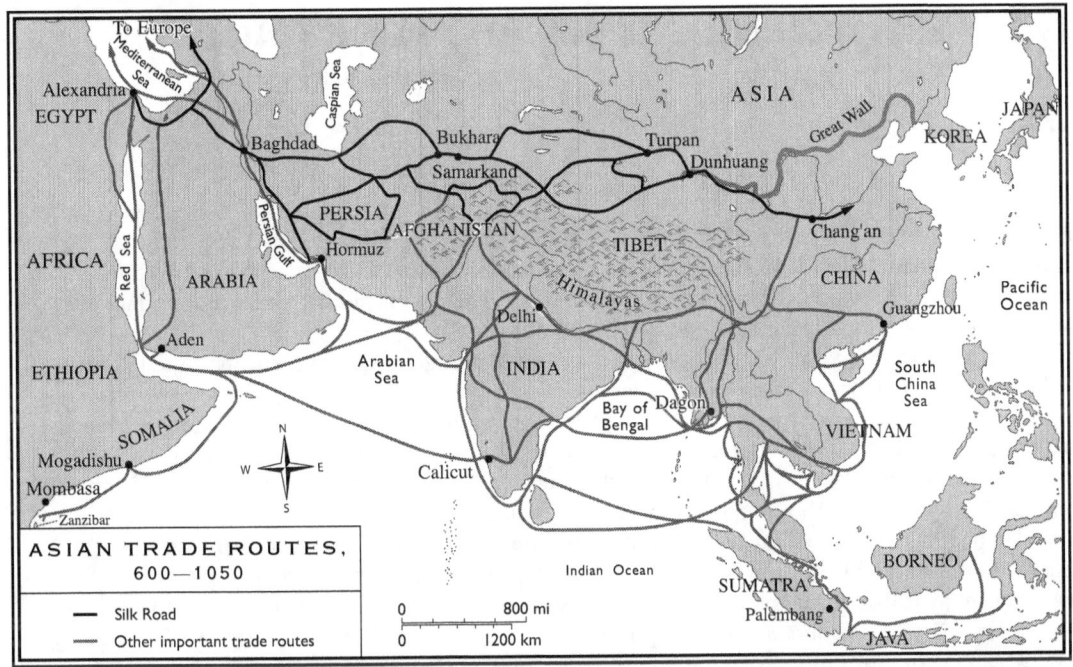

1. At which cities did the Silk Road intersect with other trade routes?

2. Why was the Silk Road so far north of India?

3. How were goods transported on the Silk Road? How was this different from transportation on the other important trade routes?

4. Would merchants need to travel the whole length of the Silk Road to profit from the trade? Explain your answer.

5. Show on the map where the following items came from, and in which direction they traveled on the Silk Road:
   a. silkworms
   b. production of silk cloth, mid-6th century
   c. paper

NAME   **DATE**

PRIMARY SOURCES

THE FAR WEST: A CHINESE DESCRIPTION OF BYZANTIUM

Directions

Read the excerpt from *The History of the Tang Dynasty*. Then answer the questions.

> The country of Fulin [Byzantium], also called Daqin [Roman Syria], is located above the western sea [Indian Ocean]. In the southeast it borders on Bosi [Persia]. . . . There are four hundred cities, and inhabited places are close together. The eaves, pillars, and window-bars of their palaces are frequently made with crystal and opaque glass.
>
> There are twelve high ministers who together are in charge of government matters. [When the king leaves the palace,] a man with a bag follows the king's carriage. Any person who has a complaint can throw a written statement into the bag. When the king comes back to the palace he decides the right and wrong of each one. Their kings are not permanent rulers, but are selected on the basis of merit. If an unusual disaster occurs in the country, or if wind and rain come at the wrong time, the king is removed and another man is put in his place. The king's cap is shaped like a bird raising its wings; its trimmings are beset with precious pearls; he wears silk-embroidered clothing, . . . He sits on a throne with golden ornaments. He has a bird like a goose; its feathers are green, and it always sits on a cushion by the side of the king. Whenever anything poisonous has been put into the king's meals, the bird will crow. The walls of their capital are built of granite, and are of enormous height. The city [Constantinople, now called Istanbul] contains in all over 100,000 households. . . . The country contains much gold, silver, and rare gems. . . . All the valuable curiosities of the West are exported from this country.

1. Do you think the person or people who wrote this description actually witnessed what they reported? Why or why not?

_____
_____
_____

2. What was unusual about the kings of Fulin and different from Chinese emperors?

_____
_____
_____

3. Why were kings removed if a natural disaster occurred in the country? Was that fair? Give reasons for your answer.

_____
_____
_____

CHAPTER TEST 4
THE ASIAN WORLD, 600–1500

NAME   **DATE**

A. MULTIPLE CHOICE

Circle the letter of the best answer to each question.

1. Which description of the Silk Road is most accurate?
   - **a.** a highway with silk fibers in it
   - **b.** a maritime route
   - **c.** a series of paths
   - **d.** a single paved road

2. Who probably carried the secret of producing silk cloth to the West?
   - **a.** Chinese silk traders
   - **b.** Xuanzang
   - **c.** Buddhist sculptors
   - **d.** Syrian Christian monks

3. When did trade in the Indian Ocean begin?
   - **a.** before the first century CE
   - **b.** before the second century CE
   - **c.** before the third century CE
   - **d.** before the fourth century CE

4. Which of the following factors had the greatest impact on trade in the Indian Ocean?
   - **a.** smuggling
   - **b.** the goods carried by ships
   - **c.** the monsoons
   - **d.** the governments

5. In what way were Sailendra and Mataram similar?
   - **a.** They are now called the Philippines.
   - **b.** They were new states in Java.
   - **c.** They were on the north coast of Borneo.
   - **d.** They were both ruled by King Airlangga.

B. SHORT ANSWER

Answer these questions in two or three sentences.

6. Explain how the monsoons affected trade to and from India.

7. Who was King Airlangga and what was his significance to trade in the Indian Ocean?

C. ESSAY

On a separate piece of paper, write an essay discussing what role the Silk Road played in the spread of ideas, beliefs, and culture. Use examples from the chapter to support your statements.

BONES AND BUDDHISTS: EARLY KOREA AND JAPAN
PAGES 66–77

FOR HOMEWORK

STUDENT STUDY GUIDE

pages 27–30

CAST OF CHARACTERS

Kim Wonjong (kim wohn-johng) king of Silla Kingdom, Korea

Sondok (sohn-duck) queen of Silla, Korea, daughter of Kim Wonjong

Prince Shotoku (show-toe-koo) Japanese co-ruler with Queen Suiko who wrote 17-article constitution

Fujiwara Michinaga (foo-jee-wah-rah mee-chee-nah-gah) head of powerful Japanese aristocratic family

Murasaki Shikibu (moo-rah-sah-kee shee-kee-boo) Japanese woman author of *The Tale of Genji*, widely recognized as the first novel

CHAPTER SUMMARY

Partly because of Buddhism, during the 6th and 7th centuries CE Korean rulers strengthened ties with China and increased their influence in Japan. In the 7th century Korea was unified under one ruler and prospered for a century and a half. Corruption among government officials led to the establishment of a new dynasty, which ruled for the next 450 years. Along with Buddhism, Confucianism took hold in Japan. Japan adopted writing from China, and China's influence could also be seen in architecture. By the early 11th century, most of Japan's people were poor, but art and literature flourished among the aristocracy. Japanese scholars had worked out a hybrid writing system and a Japanese woman had written the first novel. In 1185 civil wars ushered in a new period in Japanese history.

PERFORMANCE OBJECTIVES

- To analyze the influence of Buddhism in Korea
- To describe Silla period in Korea
- To analyze the influences of Buddhism and Confucianism in Japan
- To identify Chinese influence in Japanese government, writing, and architecture
- To describe the Nara and Heian periods in Japan

BUILDING BACKGROUND

Ask students to preview the chapter by reading the headings and subheadings, studying the photographs and captions, and examining the map on page 66. Based on the preview, work with students to compile a list of questions about what was going on in Japan and Korea between 100 and 1500. As students answer these questions in the course of studying the chapter, have them record their answers in their history journals.

VOCABULARY

aristocracy class of people that rules by inheritance

status position in relation to others

succession the sequence in which people get to rule

doctrines beliefs that are largely unquestioned

oppressing keeping down by force

lacquer a glossy material from the lacquer tree

hybrid something that combines parts of two different things

50 | CHAPTER 5

WORKING WITH PRIMARY SOURCES

Have a volunteer read aloud the excerpt from *The Tale of Genji* on page 60 of *The Medieval & Early Modern World Primary Sources and Reference Volume*. In this excerpt, Genji describes the power of fiction. Begin a discussion of the passage by asking, Do you agree with Genji that even though the reader knows that a work of fiction is made up, he or she can get completely swept up in it anyway? Does Genji seem like an actual person? Why or why not? After discussing the excerpt, tell students that they will read another excerpt from *The Tale of Genji* at the end of the chapter.

GEOGRAPHY CONNECTION

Region Have students identify China, Japan, and Korea (today consisting of the states of North and South Korea) on a world map. Compare the size and location of the regions. Point out Korea's location between China and Japan. Explain that although Korea was much smaller than China or Japan, it was a crucial link between the two regions because of its location right between them: anyone wanting to travel to Japan from China would most likely go through Korea to avoid a long sea voyage across the Sea of Japan. Ask students how they think Buddhism spread from China to Japan. *(through travelers from China who passed through Korea and came to Japan)*

READING COMPREHENSION QUESTIONS

1. How did the attitude about women rulers differ between China and Korea? *(China believed that women rulers were possible but unnatural, but Korea was more accepting of them.)*
2. For what purpose did the state of Silla use force and diplomacy in the 7th century? *(the defeat of Koguryo and Paekche and the unification of Korea)*
3. Why did Silla's power begin to decline during the 9th century? *(Disputes over succession weakened royal authority; corruption of officials led to huge fortunes, while common people suffered and rebelled.)*
4. What was Prince Shotoku's political purpose in issuing the constitution? *(to establish his sister's position as head of state with the sole right to collect taxes)*
5. In what ways was the Japanese capital of Nara similar to and different from the Chinese capital of Chang'an? *(Nara had streets laid out in a grid, the palace was in the northern part of the city, the Buddhist temples and palaces were built in Chinese style, but, unlike cities in China, Nara was not surrounded by a defensive wall.)*
6. What system of government developed in Heian? *(The emperor shared power with the most important aristocratic families.)*
7. How did the lives of the Heian aristocracy differ from that of the common people in early 11th century Japan? *(The aristocracy, including noble women, were rich and highly educated, whereas farmers and most other commoners were poor and illiterate.)*

CRITICAL THINKING QUESTIONS

1. Why was the writing of Murasaki Shikibu so important? *(Possible answer: She invented a new and very influential form, the novel, with fully developed characters and a plot.)*
2. How adept was the Fujiwara family at politics? Why do you think so? *(Possible answer: very adept because the family worked out a system to keep themselves in power by forcing the emperors to marry Fujiwara daughters.)*
3. Do you agree with the idea expressed in Heian art that the beauty of things (such as cherry blossoms) is enhanced by their short lives? Give reasons for your answer. *(Answers will vary.)*

THEN and NOW

Just as in the 6th through 12th centuries, contemporary Japan has an emperor. As in much of that earlier period, the Japanese emperor is a symbol of the state while real authority is held by others, in this case today by a prime minister from a single dominant party.

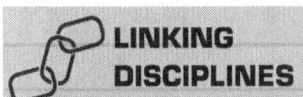
LINKING DISCIPLINES

Architecture Have students do research to find out how a key theme of Heian art, *mono no aware*, "the fragility of things," is expressed in visual arts and in literature. Encourage them to share what they learn with their classmates by displaying examples or reading poems.

LITERATURE CONNECTION

Jones, Susan W., trans. *Ages Ago: Thirty-seven Tales from the Konjaku Monogatari Collection.* Harvard University Press, 1959. Konjaku Monogatari, or Konjaku stories, are folktales from the Heian period in Japan. Students may be surprised that the stories, begin with the same phrase, "Ima wa Mukashi," which means "once upon a time."

SOCIAL SCIENCES

Economics Have students debate the advantages and disadvantages of having a single strong emperor. Ask the students to weigh the relationship between peace and prosperity in the various periods of Japanese history. One answer might be that there are different kinds of prosperity—agricultural, commercial, etc.—and different levels of wealth among different groups (or classes) of people.

READING AND LANGUAGE ARTS

Reading Nonfiction Ask students to use the main idea map (see reproducibles at the back of this guide) to help them understand a dense or difficult paragraph in the chapter. Model the procedure by identifying the main idea in the second paragraph (*Queen Sondok was an able ruler in Korea*) and having volunteers suggest important supporting details (*forming a strong alliance with China; building an astronomical observatory*). Urge students to add as many details to the map as necessary to record all the significant details in the paragraph they choose.

Using Language Write the names *Buddha* and *Confucius* on the board and have a volunteer identify their part of speech (*proper noun*). Let students find proper nouns and adjectives in the chapter, for example, *Buddhist*, that are derived from these words and explain how the spelling of the name changes. Remind students that proper nouns and proper adjectives refer to specific people, places, things, and ideas and are capitalized.

WRITING

Have students write a summary of the influence of Buddhism and of Confucianism on the constitution that Prince Shotoku issued. Ask: Which parts were more influenced by Buddhism, and which parts display more evidence of Confucian ideas?

SUPPORTING LEARNING

English Language Learners Read aloud the chapter to the group and sum up the first two paragraphs by explaining that the chapter begins by describing Kim Wonjong of Silla in Korea and his daughter Sondok. Write the names on the board. Then read aloud the first two paragraphs of the chapter and discuss them with students. Have students turn to the headings in the chapter. Explain that Nara and Heian were periods in Japanese history that were named after cities. Let pairs of students read the rest of the chapter, stopping after each section to discuss it and try to figure out parts that puzzled them. Circulate among students to answer questions.

Struggling Readers Encourage students to use sticky notes to mark words in the text that they can't figure out from context, ideas that don't make sense to them, and the names of people and places that they want to remember. Have students review the notes after they finish reading the chapter. Let them work in small groups to figure out unknown words and unclear ideas.

EXTENDING LEARNING

Enrichment Encourage students to read more of *The Tale of Genji*. After they finish reading substantial portions of the novel, ask students to imagine that they are Japanese literary critics of the Heian period who have just read this innovative work. Have them write book reviews of *The Tale of Genji*.

Extension Ask students to take the part of one of the rulers discussed in the chapter. Have them write and perform a monologue as that ruler. In their monologue they should introduce themselves to the class and tell about their greatest joys and achievements.

LITERACY TIPS

In addition to using the suggestions in the Supporting Learning and Extending Learning sections, refer back frequently to pages 16–19 for strategies and advice from a literacy coach.

NAME   **DATE**

A BOY BECOMES A MAN

Directions

Read the excerpt from *The Tale of Genji*. Then answer the questions.

> His Majesty was reluctant to spoil Genji's boyish charm, but in Genji's twelfth year he gave him his coming of age, busying himself personally with the preparations and adding new embellishments to the ceremony. Lest the event seem less imposing than the one for the Heir Apparent, done some years ago in the Shishiden [Palace], and lest anything go amiss, he issued minute instructions for the banquets. . . .
>
> He had his throne face east from the outer, eastern chamber of his residence, with the seats for the young man and his sponsor, the Minister, before him. Genji appeared at the hour of the Monkey [4:00 p.m.]. His Majesty appeared to regret that Genji would never again look as he did now, with his hair tied in twin [ponytails] and his face radiant with the freshness of youth. The Lord of the Treasury and the Chamberlain did their duty. The Lord of the Treasury was plainly sorry to cut off such beautiful hair, and His Majesty, who wished desperately that [Genji's mother] might have been there to see it, needed the greatest self-mastery not to weep.
>
> All present shed tears when, after donning the headdress and withdrawing to the anteroom, Genji then appeared in the robes of a man and stepped down into the garden to salute his Sovereign. His Majesty, of course, was still more deeply moved, and in his mind he sadly reviewed the past, when the boy's mother had been such a comfort to him. He had feared that Genji's looks might suffer once his hair was put up, at least while he remained so young, but not at all: he only looked more devastatingly handsome than ever.

1. What kind of celebration does this passage describe?

2. Why is everyone so upset?

3. What is the most likely reason that Genji's mother is not present to witness the ceremony?

PRIMARY SOURCES

Directions

Read the quotations. Then answer the questions.

> Serve your sovereign with loyalty; attend your parents with filial piety; treat your friends with sincerity; do not retreat from a battlefield; be discriminating about the taking of life.
> —Korean Buddhist monk Wongwang, in his essay, "Five Principles," 608

> When those above are harmonious and those below are friendly . . . what is there which cannot be accomplished?
> —Article I of Prince Shotoku's 17-article constitution, 604

> Nothing can be worse than allowing the driver of one's ox-carriage to be badly dressed.
> —Sei Shonagon, Heian period court lady, from her memoir *The Pillow Book*, about 1030

> On a spring hillside I took lodging for the night; and as I slept the blossoms kept falling—even in the midst of my dreams.
> —Heian poet Ki no Tsurayuki, "Spring," about 900

1. Which quotation reflects the idea of *mono no aware*, or the fragility of things?

2. Which quotation says something about aristocratic lifestyles?

3. Which values are expressed in the quotations?

4. Which values do you agree with? Give reasons. Are there any values you don't agree with? Why?

5. What values not mentioned in the quotations do you think are important for virtuous living and a good society?

CHAPTER TEST 5

THE ASIAN WORLD, 600–1500

A. MULTIPLE CHOICE

Circle the letter of the best answer to each question.

1. Why did Sondok inherit the throne from Kim Wonjong of Silla?
   a. She led a rebellion and killed the king.
   b. She was his wife, so Kim Wonjong appointed her.
   c. She was elected by the aristocracy.
   d. There was no male heir.

2. Why did relations between the court and temples come to a crisis under Empress Koken?
   a. She was too cruel a ruler.
   b. The monks didn't want an empress.
   c. Powerful families opposed the influences of commoner monks.
   d. She was incompetent.

3. In the Heian period, with whom did the emperor share power?
   a. his counselors
   b. Buddhist monks
   c. the queen
   d. the aristocracy

4. During the 11th century, what were most Japanese people?
   a. aristocrats
   b. farmers
   c. merchants
   d. servants

5. Who was Genji in *The Tale of Genji*?
   a. a queen
   b. a Buddhist monk
   c. an imperial prince
   d. a visitor from Korea

B. SHORT ANSWER

Answer these questions in two or three sentences.

6. Explain why Silla power declined in the 9th century.

7. How did the Fujiwara family weaken the state and eventually bring the Heian period to an end?

C. ESSAY

On a separate piece of paper, write a short essay comparing the Nara and Heian periods in Japan. Use details from the chapter to support your statements.

CHAPTER 6

HORSEMEN AND GENTLEMEN: THE SONG DYNASTY IN CHINA
PAGES 78–90

FOR HOMEWORK

STUDENT STUDY GUIDE

pages 31–34

CAST OF CHARACTERS

Yelü Abaoji (YEH-lew ah-BAOW-jee) Khitan ruler, founder and first emperor of Liao dynasty

Zhao Kuangyin (jao kwong-yin) founder of Song dynasty, also known as Song Taizu (suhng-tie-dzoo)

Zhu Xi (joo syee) Song dynasty scholar and philosopher

Fan Kuan (fahn kwahn) Song dynasty landscape painter who became a Daoist hermit

Li Qingzhao (lee ching-jao) (1084–c.1151) Song dynasty woman poet

CHAPTER SUMMARY

In 960 Zhao Kuangyin established the Song dynasty, which controlled much of China except the northeast, which was controlled by the Liao dynasty, and the northwest, which was controlled by the Xixia kingdom. The scholar-official class had new power, which stemmed from education. Early in the 12th century the Liao dynasty was replaced by the Jin dynasty, which encroached into Song land, forcing the Song government to move south to a new seaport capital. Maritime trade expanded, prompting improvements in shipbuilding and navigation. New weapons used gunpowder, and new farming techniques increased food-growing capacity. Urban life, art, and literature flourished. Confucian ideas kept women subservient, and binding women's feet became prevalent.

PERFORMANCE OBJECTIVES

- To identify the Liao, Xixia, and Jin dynasties
- To analyze characteristics of the Song dynasty such as the rise of the scholar-official class and the examination system
- To describe Song dynasty improvements in shipbuilding, navigation, weaponry, and farming
- To analyze new ideas in philosophy and religion
- To describe urban, artistic, and intellectual life
- To analyze the status of women during the Song dynasty

BUILDING BACKGROUND

Remind students that though the vast majority (more than 90 percent) of Chinese are Han, the Chinese people today comprise more than 50 ethnic groups, each with its own regional association, language, customs, and identity. Have students tell what they know of any of the various ethnic groups in today's China. Explain that in this chapter, students will read about the Khitan, Tangut, and Jurchen people of northern China during the 10th to 13th centuries.

VOCABULARY

emulate try to copy

encroach expand one's power or possessions at the expense of another

masts vertical poles on the deck of ships that support sails and rigging

rudders vertically hinged plates that direct the course of vessels

suspended hung so as to allow free movement

catapults military machines for hurling missiles

modify change

hermit a person who withdraws from society and lives alone

WORKING WITH PRIMARY SOURCES

Ask students to skim the chapter to identify primary source material. Have them explain how they know that these passages are from primary sources (*quotation marks that indicate the actual words a person said or wrote and source citations*) and what such passages add to their understanding of ancient times and distant places. Encourage students to read aloud some of the quotations in the chapter.

READING COMPREHENSION QUESTIONS

1. What did the Khitan and Tangut rulers think of the Han Chinese? (*Possible answer: They thought the Chinese were soft and timid.*)
2. How did the Song rulers maintain peace on China's borders in the 10th and 11th centuries? (*by diplomacy and sharing resources, transfers of wealth*)
3. What was key to the rise of the scholar-official class? (*the examination system*)
4. What was education like during the Song dynasty? (*Possible answer: It depended on tutors and required studying the Confucian classics, applying their principles to contemporary problems, and practicing writing Chinese characters beautifully.*)
5. Why did the Song capital move south? (*The Jin dynasty began encroaching into Song territory and defeated the Song, who were led by a weak leader.*)
6. What effects did the new seaport capital cause? (*Trade increased and led to improvements in shipbuilding and navigation.*)
7. What did Kaifeng and Lin'an (Hangzhou) have in common? (*They were both big cities of about one million people.*)
8. Why was foot binding invented, and why did it remain popular for so long in China? (*Possible answer: It was thought to be beautiful, it kept women at home, and it was considered the sign of a civilized society.*)

CRITICAL THINKING QUESTIONS

1. Why do you think exposure to Buddhism led Chinese scholars such as Zhu Xi to examine Confucianism more closely? (*Possible answer: they believed the Confucianism was the best way to create a well-governed society, but they understood that Buddhism offered a more satisfying spiritual life, so they reinterpreted Confucianism in a way that emphasized spiritual values.*)
2. What might have been one message of Fan Kuan's paintings? (*Possible answer: that human beings should try to fit harmoniously into the natural world, rather than seek to dominate nature*)
3. Why might footbinding have been considered a status symbol at first? (*Possible answer: Because only rich families could afford to do without the labor power of their women.*)

SOCIAL SCIENCES

Economics Have students discuss how the economy of the Song dynasty changed after 1127 when the capital moved south to Lin'an. Ask: How did economic pressure after the relocation of the capital encourage inventions and improvements?

THEN and NOW

In the 12th century, the magnetic compass made ocean navigation more accurate. Inventions have continued to make navigating the seas safer and easier. These days, with the help of computers, ships can avoid obstacles, hold a course, and steer themselves!

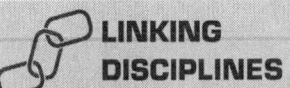

LINKING DISCIPLINES

Science Let students work together in pairs or small groups to research the Chinese compass. Ask students to demonstrate for an audience how the Chinese compass worked using visual aids or by constructing an actual compass.

THE ASIAN WORLD, 600–1500

LITERATURE CONNECTION

Poems of the Masters: China's Classic Anthology of Tang and Sung Dynasty Verse. Trans. Red Pine. Copper Canyon Press, 2003. Poetry is China's most celebrated art, and this collection testifies to this fact. Over one hundred poets are represented in this bilingual edition, including many of China's celebrated poets: Li Pai, Wang Wei, Tu Fu, Wang Po, and Ou-yang Hsiu.

LITERACY TIPS

In addition to using the suggestions in the Supporting Learning and Extending Learning sections, refer back frequently to pages 16–19 for strategies and advice from a literacy coach.

READING AND LANGUAGE ARTS

Reading Nonfiction Let students skim the chapter to glean some ideas about what they will read. Have them read the chapter and map titles, the headings, and the captions. Ask them to look closely at illustrations, photographs, maps, and other special features. Have students jot down in their history journal some predictions about the topics they think will be included in this chapter. Encourage students to return to the predictions after they finish reading the chapter to find out how accurate they were.

Using Language Remind students that all words have denotations, or literal meanings. Many words also have connotations, or emotional associations. For example, *slender* has a very different—and more pleasing—connotation than *skinny*. Ask students to find words with positive or negative associations in the chapter *(collapsed, hurled)* and caution them to choose words carefully when they write to make sure the words have appropriate connotations.

WRITING

Have students describe the opinion of the (Han) Chinese shared by Khitan and Tangut rulers. Ask students to base their descriptions on the quotations by the rulers of these ethnic groups cited in the first and third paragraphs of the chapter.

SUPPORTING LEARNING

English Language Learners Pair students who are learning English with students whose first language is English. Have pairs read the chapter section by section. After they finish reading each section silently, have them discuss it. Urge English language learners to ask their partners to define words and explain expressions they don't understand.

Struggling Readers Introduce the chapter to students by reading aloud the title and headings. Then list on the board the other dynasties and peoples mentioned *(Liao dynasty—Khitan people, Xixia—Tangut people, Jin dynasty—Jurchen people).* Read aloud the first three paragraphs and discuss them with students. Then let students read the rest of the chapter independently.

EXTENDING LEARNING

Enrichment Let small groups of students work together to create a mural depicting urban life during the Song dynasty. Encourage students to make the mural as accurate and detailed as they can by gathering information from primary sources such as Zhang Zeduan's scroll *Going up the River in the Qing Ming Festival* and from Meng Yuanlao's memoirs.

Extension Have students use the Venn diagram graphic organizer (see reproducibles at the back of this guide) to list likenesses and differences between education in the United States of America and education in Song dynasty China. After they complete the diagram, ask students to use the Venn diagram to help them write a short paragraph comparing the goals, structure, and content of the two educational systems.

NAME   **DATE**

THE NORTHERN SONG DYNASTY, 960–1126

Directions
Complete the map to show the extent of land controlled by the Northern Song dynasty. Then answer the questions.

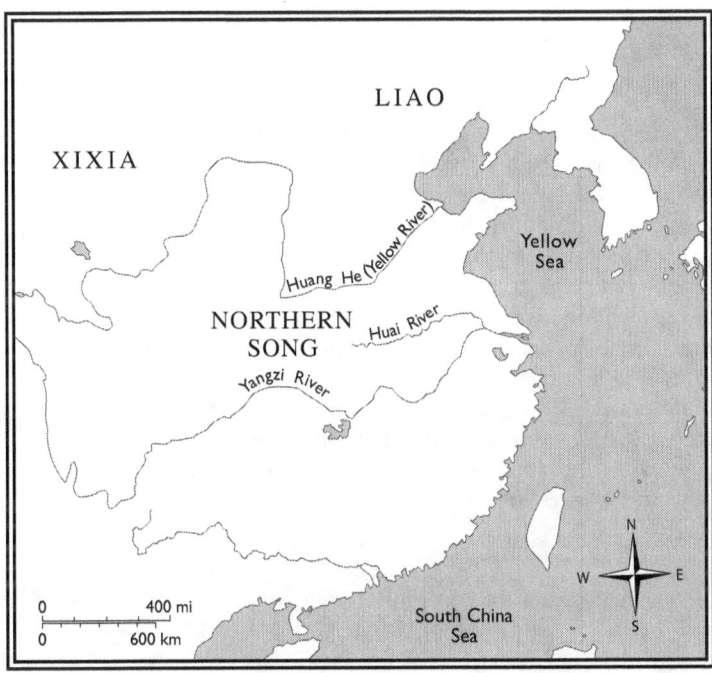

1. Locate and label the cities Yanjing and Kaifeng.

2. Use shading or a pattern to show how far the land controlled by the Northern Song dynasty extended. Make a legend next to the map to explain the shading.

3. Identify which city Zhau Kuangyin made his capital after he established his dynasty. Put a circle around the name of this city on the map.

4. What payment did Zhau make to the Liao leadership to the north to keep the peace? Write your answer on the map, with arrows showing that this payment went from the Song to the Liao.

5. How else did the Song ease relations with the Liao?
   _____
   _____

6. What did the Song leadership send to the Xixia dynasty to the west to keep peace? Write your answer on the map, using arrows to show where the payment came from and was sent.

PRIMARY SOURCES

THE ART OF BAMBOO

Directions

Read the excerpt from Su Shi's "Essay on the Bamboo Paintings of Wen Tong." Then answer the questions.

> When bamboo first grow, they are sprouts only an inch long, yet all their joints and leaves are already complete. They pass from shedding their sheaths, like cicada husks and snakeskins, and reach a point when they thrust up like swords ten yards high: this occurs as something innate within them. Nowadays painters do them joint by joint and accumulate their foliage leaf by leaf—and there is nothing left of a bamboo in it! The reason is that in order to paint bamboo, the painter must get the bamboo beforehand in his heart; then, when he takes hold of the brush and looks fully, he actually sees what he wants to paint and quickly sets out in its pursuit, and it is completed with a flourish of the brush, in which he goes after what he has seen like a falcon swooping down on a bounding hare—if you go off just a little, it gets away. This is what Wen Tong taught me. I could not do this, yet I recognized that it was true. When the mind has recognized how something is true, yet it is unable to do it, the internal and the external are not the same; mind and hand do not respond to one another, which is an error of inadequate learning. . . . This goes beyond the question of bamboo.

1. How would you sum up what Su Shi learned from Wen Tong?

2. In what way is bamboo like cicadas and snakes?

3. To what does the author compare a skilled painter? Does that comparison make sense to you? Why or why not?

4. What does the author mean in the last two sentences of the excerpt?

CHAPTER TEST 6

THE ASIAN WORLD, 600–1500

NAME _____ DATE _____

A. MULTIPLE CHOICE

Circle the letter of the best answer to each question.

1. Why did Song rulers give silk and money to the Liao?
   a. because the Song admired the Liao
   b. because the Liao traded things from the Song
   c. because the Song did not want the Liao to attack
   d. because the Song liked to pay tribute to foreigners

2. Which was **not** a feature of the Song examination system?
   a. Exams were held every three years.
   b. Few candidates were allowed to pass at each level.
   c. Successful candidates were often from poor families.
   d. A good education was necessary to pass the exams.

3. By what name is the period from 1127 to the end of the Song dynasty known?
   a. Northern Song
   b. Southern Song
   c. Eastern Song
   d. Western Song

4. What was one way the compass helped Chinese navigators?
   a. It made navigation quicker.
   b. It helped locate the stars.
   c. It made navigation more interesting.
   d. It made navigation more reliable.

5. What is the best description of Song intellectual Zhu Xi?
   a. Confucian
   b. Neo-Confucian
   c. Buddhist
   d. Daoist

6. What effect did Confucian morality have on the status of women?
   a. It improved women's lives.
   b. It could be interpreted to justify men's control over women.
   c. It gave women more personal freedom.
   d. It did not affect women's status at all.

B. SHORT ANSWER

Answer these questions in two or three sentences.

7. How did the decline of the Northern Song in 1127 affect Chinese traders?

_____
_____
_____

8. What innovation in agriculture developed under the Southern Song dynasty?

_____
_____
_____

C. ESSAY

On a separate sheet of paper, write a short essay in which you try to persuade the Song Chinese to give up the practice of footbinding. Use what you know about the values and beliefs of the Song to make a case that appeals to common values and emotions.

CHAPTER 7
KHANS AND CONQUEST: THE MONGOL EMPIRE,
PAGES 91–101

FOR HOMEWORK
STUDENT STUDY GUIDE
pages 35–38

CAST OF CHARACTERS

Genghis Khan (JENG-hiz kahn) (c. 1160–1227) Mongol world conqueror; original name Temujin (Teh-moo-jin)

Ho'elun (HOH eh-luhn) mother of Genghis Khan

Borte wife of Genghis Khan

Qiu Chuji (chyoh choo-jee) Chinese Daoist priest who visited Genghis Khan

Jochi (JOH-chee) eldest son of Genghis Khan

Ogodei (OH-go-day) son of Genghis Khan, Great Khan 1229–1241

Mongke (MUNG-kay) grandson of Genghis Khan, Great Khan

Khubilai Khan (KOO-buh-lie kahn) grandson of Genghis Khan, founded Yuan dynasty of China

Rashid al-Din (Rah-SHEED ahl-DEEN) Muslim statesman and historian

CHAPTER SUMMARY

The great Mongol leader Temujin, or Genghis Khan ("Universal Leader"), united tribes of the steppes of Central Asia and created a permanent military of frightening efficiency. Beginning in 1206, he extended his rule into China, India, Persia, and Russia, but was unable to create permanent government institutions in conquered lands. His successors briefly forged an empire that extended into Eastern Europe and the Middle East. By 1253, when Genghis's descendent Khubilai was leading military expeditions in China (which he would later rule as emperor), the Mongol Empire was already beginning to lose its unity and would soon fragment into four separate parts.

PERFORMANCE OBJECTIVES

► To describe Genghis Khan's early life and rise to power
► To analyze Genghis Khan's achievements and failures
► To understand the nature of tribal society
► To understand the Mongols' motivation for conquest
► To summarize the actions and achievements of Genghis Khan's successors

BUILDING BACKGROUND

Ask students what image comes to mind when they hear the name Genghis Khan. Have them think of as many words as they can to describe this great—and notoriously ruthless—ruler. Ask a volunteer to write the descriptive words the class suggests on the board. Urge students to look at the list again after they finish reading the chapter to decide which words they would remove and which new ones they would add after learning more about Genghis Khan.

VOCABULARY

clan division of a tribe that comes from a common ancestor
confederation group of allies united for a common purpose
plunder robbery or taking goods by force
suppress put down by force
humility quality of being meek or modest

WORKING WITH PRIMARY SOURCES

Read aloud to the class the two different impressions of the Mongols in the chapter: from Chinese Daoist priest, Qiu Chuji (see page 96) and from English historian Matthew Paris (see page 99). Compare the two excerpts, and discuss the point of view of each writer. Ask the following: What were the authors' backgrounds? Might either of them have had a bias for or against the Mongols? Did they witness the events they wrote about? How can we evaluate the accuracy of accounts like these?

GEOGRAPHY CONNECTION

Region Describe to students the steppe where the Mongols originated. Identify Mongolia on the map on pages 14–15 and explain that the steppe was a vast plain stretching across Central Asia. Because of light rainfall, the area has few trees and is not suitable for farming. Ask students how people would have to live to survive in such an environment (*They would have to be nomadic because conditions didn't allow for farming; horses would be important for moving from place to place.*)

READING COMPREHENSION QUESTIONS

1. By what name do people today know Temujin? (*Genghis Khan*)
2. What was Mongol life of the 12th century like? (*The Mongols raised and rode horses, lived in tents of felt, drank fermented mares' milk, and believed in the power of shamans; after the 1140s, they grew poor.*)
3. What were Temujin's abilities and personal qualities that contributed to his success? (*He could ride, hunt, and fight. He was competitive, ambitious and a natural leader.*)
4. How do members of a tribe treat one another? (*as relatives*)
5. What must a tribal society do to be successful? (*operate successfully at the family, clan, tribal, and confederation levels.*)
6. What kept Genghis Khan's troops loyal? (*his success in battle*)
7. What problem could Genghis Khan not overcome after he conquered a land? (*He could not create permanent government institutions.*)
8. How did Yelü Chucai, a Khiton-Chinese nobleman, justify working for the conquering Mongols? (*He felt that by persuading the Mongols to rule with Chinese methods, he was shielding his people from the harshest effects of Mongol rule.*)

CRITICAL THINKING QUESTIONS

1. How might the environment in which the Mongols lived have contributed to their behavior as warriors? (*Possible answer: Only the strong could survive successfully in such a harsh environment, so it was understandable that they were fierce and pitiless fighters.*)
2. Was it justifiable for Temujin's relatives to abandon him and his family? Give reasons for your answer. (*Students may answer yes because their first duty was to survive or no because deserting the family was too disloyal no matter what the circumstances.*)
3. How do we know that the Mongols thought Genghis Khan was a great leader? (*Possible answer: The Mongol tribes would not have followed him into battle as enthusiastically as they did, as demonstrated by his title, which translates as "universal leader."*)

SOCIAL SCIENCES

Civics Distribute the main idea map graphic organizer (see reproducibles at the back of this guide). Let students use this graphic organizer to describe how the tribal societies of the Mongol Empire functioned. Have them write *Tribal Societies* in the center oval. Then have students sum up what they learned about this topic in the detail ovals of the map. Encourage students to add as many detail ovals as they need to.

THEN and NOW

After weakening in the 13th century, The Mongol states began to break apart in the 14th century. The Mongols eventually came under strong Chinese influence, which lasted many centuries. With Soviet help, Mongolia won its independence in 1921. The Mongolian People's Revolutionary Party has led a coalition government in Mongolia since 2004.

LINKING DISCIPLINES

Mathematics Have students figure out how many square miles the Mongol Empire encompassed at its most powerful. Then have them find out the size of the independent state of Mongolia today. Ask students to compare mathematically the size of the Mongol Empire in its heyday to Mongolia today.

THE ASIAN WORLD, 600–1500

LITERATURE CONNECTION

Carpini, Giovanni di Plano. *The Story of the Mongols Whom We Call the Tartars: Friar Giovanni di Plano Carpini's Account of His Embassy to the Court of the Mongol Khan.* Branden Books, 1996. Nonfiction. A friar sent by the pope to learn more about the Mongols provided this first-person account. ADVANCED

Dion, Frederick. *The Blue Wolf: The Epic Tale of the Life of Genghis Khan and the Empire of the Steppes.* Thomas Dunne Books, 2003. Historical Fiction. This story focuses on Genghis Khan's rise to power. ADVANCED

Khan, Paul. *Secret History of the Mongols: The Origin of Chingis Khan.* Cheng & Tsui, 1999. Poetry. Based on a translation, this narrative poem gives the Mongols' perspective on the rise of their nation. AVERAGE

LITERACY TIPS

In addition to using the suggestions in the Supporting Learning and Extending Learning sections, refer back frequently to pages 16–19 for strategies and advice from a literacy coach.

READING AND LANGUAGE ARTS

Reading Nonfiction Remind students that features often found in works of nonfiction can help them understand what they read. Point out the photo captions, words in italics and boldfaced type, and headings. Ask: What topics would you expect to read about under the three headings in this chapter: Tribes and Power, From Plunder to Empire, and The Heirs of Genghis Khan? Note that headings not only give a snapshot of the information that follows but also break up lengthy text and make it less intimidating.

Using Language Have students develop fluent reading by using context to figure out the meaning of unknown words. Ask students to find several words in the chapter whose exact meanings puzzle them. Let students use context, the other words in the sentence and the sentences before and after the one with the unknown word, to develop hypotheses about the meanings of these words. Then have them check the meanings in a dictionary and compare their working definition with the dictionary definition.

WRITING

Expository Paragraph Have students write a one-paragraph explanation of how Genghis Khan rose to power, how tribal societies were organized, or the significance of Genghis Kahn's successors. Ask students to include a topic sentence, supporting sentences, and a conclusion in their paragraph.

SUPPORTING LEARNING

English Language Learners Read up to the first heading aloud to students to introduce them to the topic and hear how some of the names they will encounter are pronounced. Stop after each paragraph and summarize its meaning. Encourage students to stop periodically as they read the remainder of the chapter independently to summarize what they read in their minds. Urge students to reread puzzling passages.

Struggling Readers Tell students that several of the people in this chapter have titles as well as given names. As they read the chapter, ask students to keep track of each new person they read about. Have them write the person's name, title if she or he has one, and a brief description of the person. Encourage students to consult their list if they forget

EXTENDING LEARNING

Enrichment Encourage students to find out about contemporary life in the steppelands of Mongolia. Have them compare and contrast life in Mongolia today with life at the time of Genghis Khan.

Extension Have students debate Genghis Khan's goals and tactics. Students on both sides of the debate should provide solid factual reasons rather than emotional responses.

THE MONGOL EMPIRE, 1206–1280

Directions
Complete the map to show the Mongol empire. Then answer the questions.

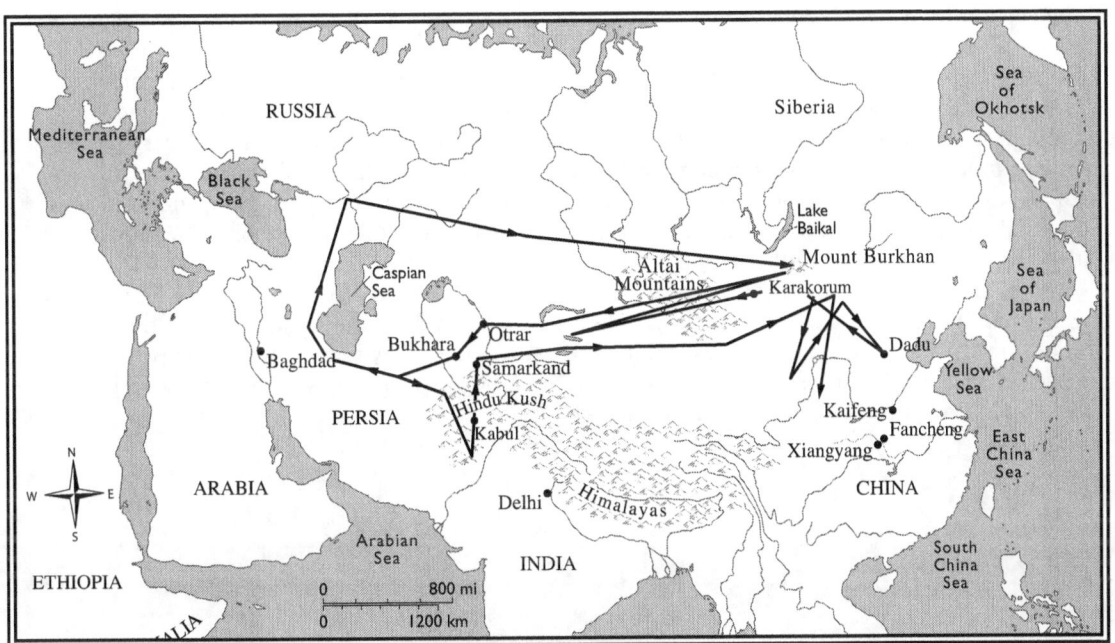

1. Use shading or a pattern to show territory conquered by the Mongols by 1227.

2. Use a different color or pattern to show territory conquered by the Mongols by 1280.

3. Create a legend to explain the patterns.

4. Identify the place where the Mongol chiefs formally recognized Genghis Khan as their leader. Draw a circle around this place on the map.

5. Which Chinese capital did Genghis Khan besiege successfully in 1215? Draw a square around the name of this city on the map.

CHAPTER 7 BLM
THE ASIAN WORLD, 600–1500

NAME   **DATE**

PRIMARY SOURCES

OGODEI KHAN SHOWS MERCY

Directions

Read the excerpt from *The Complete Collection of Histories* by Rashid al-Din. Then answer the questions.

> According to the *yasa*, it is forbidden for anyone to bathe or wash clothes in running water. One day some Mongol guardsmen saw a Muslim bathing in a stream; they seized him and brought him before the Great Khan Ogodei for sentencing. But the Great Khan felt sorry for the man, condemned by a law of which he was ignorant. Speaking to the Muslim in private, the Great Khan told him to plead that he was a pauper and, having accidentally dropped his last piece of silver, he waded in to find it. Then the Great Khan secretly sent one of his servants to throw a piece of silver into the stream.
>
> The next morning, the case was heard in court. The Muslim told the story as the Great Khan had instructed him. The Great Khan then sent his guards to the stream to see if they could find evidence that the man was telling the truth. When they returned with the piece of silver, the Great Khan pardoned the Muslim for violating the *yasa*, and sent him away with a reward of ten additional pieces of silver for his trouble.

1. What was the purpose of the *yasa*?

2. Why did the Muslim break the law, and how did the Great Kahn feel about the man's behavior?

3. What did you think of the Great Kahn's solution to the problem?

CHAPTER TEST 7
THE ASIAN WORLD, 600–1500

NAME _____ **DATE** _____

A. MULTIPLE CHOICE

Circle the letter of the best answer to each question.

1. What did Temujin's relatives do after the boy's father died?
   a. They adopted him.
   b. They murdered him.
   c. They joined another tribe.
   d. They hunted down the father's killers.

2. At what skill was Temujin **not** exceptional?
   a. peace-making
   b. hunting
   c. fighting
   d. leading

3. What is a tribe?
   a. a group of people who exchange goods
   b. a group of people who live near each other
   c. a group of people who form a confederation
   d. a group of people who cooperate as a society

4. What word **best** describes the army of Genghis Khan?
   a. modern
   b. efficient
   c. unusual
   d. trustworthy

5. What was significant about the Mongol army conquering the city of Zhongdu?
   a. Zhongdu was the Jin capital
   b. Zhongdu was the largest city the Mongol's had fought.
   c. Zhongdu was the first Chinese city the army had beaten.
   d. Zhongdu was within the Great Wall.

6. Which of Genghis Kahn's descendants was his immediate successor?
   a. Jochi
   b. Khubilai
   c. Ogodei
   d. Mongke

B. SHORT ANSWER
Answer these questions in two or three sentences.

7. Was Genghis Khan able to establish a stable empire after he conquered a territory? Explain your answer.
   _____
   _____

8. How did Ghenghis Khan advance against the Jurchen Jin dynasty from 1212 to 1215?
   _____
   _____

C. CHART
Complete the chart by writing an effect of each cause.

CAUSE	EFFECT
1. In the 1140s the Mongols lost battles against the neighboring Tatars.	
2. Temujin's father accepted hospitality from a group of Tatars.	
3. Temujin raided the herds of neighboring tribes.	
4. Temujin became incredibly successful in battle and in gathering followers who accepted his leadership.	
5. Uighur scholars figured out a way to write the Mongol language.	
6. A Khwarazmi governor slaughtered a caravan of Mongol envoys and traders.	
7. Yelü convinced the Mongol leaders to tax instead of plunder.	

CHAPTER 8

SULTANS, SLAVES, AND SOUTHERNERS: THE SULTANATE OF DELHI IN INDIA PAGES 102–112

FOR HOMEWORK

STUDENT STUDY GUIDE

pages 39–42

CAST OF CHARACTERS

Qutb-ud-din Aybak (KUTB-ood-deen AYE-bahk) first sultan of Delhi

Raziya (RAHZ-ee-yah) third Sultan of Delhi, India and only woman to be sultan

Ala-ud-din Khalji (ah-lah-ood-deen CALL-jee) sultan of Delhi

Tughluq former slave who became sultan in 1316 and was possibly killed by his son

Muhammad bin Tughluq (mu-HAM-mahd bin TOOG-luck) sultan of Delhi known as "The Bloody Sultan"

Abu 'Abdallah ibn Battuta or **Ibn Battuta** (IB-en bah-TOO-tah) Arab traveler and writer

Timer Leng (TEE-mur lung) Central Asian conqueror known in Europe as Tamerlane

Kabir (kah-BEER) Indian mystic and poet

CHAPTER SUMMARY

The rulers of the Delhi sultanate in India did not have to be born into royalty. Some rulers began as slaves and were later named sultan. Some of the sultans ruled ruthlessly, instilling fear in their subjects. During the rule of these Muslim sultans, Islam continued to spread and many Hindus converted to Islam. Muslim culture was also influential in the areas of music and dress.

PERFORMANCE OBJECTIVES

- To identify the rulers of the Delphi sultanate
- To describe the relationship between the Hindus and the Muslims in India between 1206 and 1500
- To understand the influence of Muslim rule and culture in India between 1206 and 1500
- To identify aspects of Hindu culture between 1206 and 1500

BUILDING BACKGROUND

Invite students to name some of the famous leaders they know of. Have them share what they know about the backgrounds and lives of these people and to discuss how these people became leaders. Explain that the chapter they will be reading is about some of the sultans in India who came from different backgrounds, whether they were born as slaves and became rulers, or were children of rulers and had the title passed on to them.

VOCABULARY

ambitious having the desire to be successful

salvaged saved from the wreckage

accommodate to make fit

successive following in order

contemporary living during the same time period

deference tendency to yield to the will of others

conscientious careful and attentive

WORKING WITH PRIMARY SOURCES

Bakhti poetry was a way for Hindu poets to express their deep feelings. One example is the poem by the poet Ratanbai in *The Medieval & Early Modern World Primary Sources and Reference Volume* (see page 61). Read the poem aloud to students and have them discuss the spiritual meaning the poet is trying to convey. Students may also be interested to know that some *bakhti* poems are set to music. Two *bakhti* poems by the female poet Mirabai (1498–1546) that have been set to music can be heard at www.anu.edu.au/asianstudies/hindi/swah2005/mirabai.html

GEOGRAPHY CONNECTION

Interaction Have the class turn to the map on page 106 in the Student Edition. Point out that the map shows different regions, and ask students how the map and legend explain these regions. Point out that by the 1300s, India was divided into a northern, Islamic, section and a Hindu section to the south, when Harihara and Bukka Sangama rebelled against the sultanate and established Vijayanagara, a new Hindu capital. Describe the geography of India and explain that these areas were separated by a large central plateau. Ask students to locate this area on the map.

READING COMPREHENSION QUESTIONS

1. How did Aybak react to Hindu life when he became the first Muslim ruler of Hindu northern India? *(Aybak got rid of many Hindu statues and had many Hindu temples destroyed. He had many Muslim mosques built but he allowed people to worship as they pleased.)*

2. What characteristics made Raziya an unusual sultan? *(She was a woman and she dressed in men's clothing.)*

3. Why was Muhammad bin Tughluq called "The Bloody Sultan"? *(He was known for his harsh punishments and had the people who displeased him killed.)*

4. What lead to the end of the Delhi Sultanate? *(Timur Leng and his soldiers attacked the city and killed all the Hindus. They took all the wealth of the city and Delhi never recovered.)*

CRITICAL THINKING QUESTIONS

1. Why was Vijayanagara important? *(Possible answers: It was a stronghold of Hindu culture and a place for Hindus to visit on pilgrimage.)*

2. How did Hindu and Muslim cultures influence each other in India? *(Possible answers: Many Hindus converted to Islam and adopted Muslim clothing and music styles. As well, intermarriage between Hindus and Muslims became more common and Muslims became more comfortable with Hindu religious practices.)*

SOCIAL SCIENCES

Civics In the 13th century it was uncommon for a woman to have political power, much less to be the leader of a sultanate. Raziya was an exception to the rule as a sultan of the Delhi Sultanate. Since the time of Raziya, many Indian women have followed in her footsteps and have been great rulers and leaders in their country. The website www.geocities.com/dakshina_kan_pa/art31/women2.htm, although way above the 7th grade level, has information for teachers about some of these women and links to information about women leaders, and warriors who have been honored on Indian postage stamps.

READING AND LANGUAGE ARTS

Reading Nonfiction Give students examples of cause-and-effect statements: *Because there was violent competition to inherit a throne, rulers in the Muslim world often trusted their slaves more than they did their own relatives.* Have partners review the chapter. One partner should write down the cause part of a sentence; the other partner should complete the sentence with the effect.

THEN and NOW

Today, in the modern nation of India, 82 percent of the population is Hindu and only 12 percent is Muslim. But many Muslims live in Pakistan and Bangladesh, countries that were part of India in medieval times. Other religions of India include Christianity, Sikhism, Buddhism, Jainism, Zoroastrianism, and Judaism.

LINKING DISCIPLINES

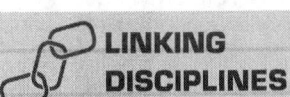

Art-Architecture Religious buildings are often designed with symbolic ideas in mind. Ask students to work in pairs to research information about each of these types of buildings and compare some of the characteristics and religious meanings of these buildings.

LITERATURE CONNECTION

Ibn Battuta on the Web offers text in translation, an overview of Ibn Battuta's travels, maps, and pictures of this legendary figures's journeys. *www.isidore-of-seville.com/ibn-battuta.*

After exploring the site with your students, ask them to write about their own exploration of these new lands, focusing on the Sultanate at Delhi.

Ali, Ahmed. *Twilight in Delhi.* New Directions, 1994. Though this is a contemporary story, set during the early years of this century, it captures the daily melody of traditional life in the old city of Delhi among the last, impoverished heirs to the refined Mogul civilization that dominated India until the advent of the English.

LITERACY TIPS

In addition to using the suggestions in the Supporting Learning and Extending Learning sections, refer back frequently to pages 16–19 for strategies and advice from a literacy coach.

Using Language The chapter contains many adjectives and descriptive phrases. Have students work with a partner to choose one person discussed in the chapter and make a list of adjectives and descriptive phrases that are used to describe this person. Then students can add their own words to the list that they think describe the person.

WRITING

Poetry Ask students to reread the poems by Kabir in the chapter. Then have them think of an important message they would like to tell people and write a four-lined *bakhti* poem about it. Students may want to share their poems with each other.

SUPPORTING LEARNING

English Language Learners Ask students to work in pairs to make a list of four or five words from the chapter that they do not know. Have them work together to figure out the meanings from context or to look up the words in the dictionary. Then have students write a sentence for each word.

Struggling Readers Have students use the timeline graphic organizer (see reproducibles at the back of this guide) to organize the information about the people and events in the chapter.

EXTENDING LEARNING

Enrichment Vijayanagara, Land of Victory, was a Hindu city-state founded after Muslim invaders were pushed out. The city survived for 200 years before falling to Muslim forces. The remains of the city are still visited by tourists and Hindus still worship at the shrines. Have students conduct an Internet search using the key word Vijayanagara. Have them print out images and information to share with classmates. Photographs of the remaining buildings and artwork, as well as maps, can be found at the website *www.cloudband.com/frames.mhtml/magazine/articles/feat_fritz_vijiyanagara_p1.html.*

Extension Have students work in pairs to make a Venn diagram to list the differences and similarities between Delhi and Vijayanagara (see reproducibles at the back of this guide). Remind students to think about the religious make-up and location as well as other characteristics of these places.

CHAPTER 8 BLM — THE ASIAN WORLD, 600–1500

NAME   **DATE**

PRIMARY SOURCES

Directions

Read the *bakhti* poem by the poet Kabir below. Then answer the questions that follow.

> As the seed contains the oil,
> And the fire's within the flint,
> So the Divine sits in the temple of yourself;
> Realize it if you can.

1. To whom is Kabir referring when he says the Divine?
   _____
   _____

2. To what is Kabir comparing the oil and the fire?
   _____
   _____

3. To what is Kabir comparing the seed and the flint?
   _____
   _____

4. What does Kabir mean by "the temple of yourself"?
   _____
   _____

5. What is Kabir asking the reader to realize?
   _____
   _____

6. On the lines below, write the poem in your own words.
   _____
   _____
   _____
   _____

PRIMARY SOURCES

Directions

Read this excerpt, and then answer the questions that follow.

> When Sultan Tughluq died his son Muhammad became master of the realm without any rival or opponent. . . . Of all the people this king loves most to give presents and also to shed blood. His door is never free from a poor person who is to be enriched and a living person who is to be killed. Stories of his generosity and bravery as well as of his cruelty and severity towards offenders are repeated widely among the people. Despite this, he is the humblest of men and the most devoted to the administration of justice and to the pursuit of truth. The sayings and principles of Islam are preserved by him. He lays great stress on the performance of prayer, and those [Muslims] who neglect to pray are punished by him. He is one of those kings whose good luck is unique and whose happy good fortune is extraordinary; but his dominating quality is his generosity.
>
> —Ibn Battuta

1. For what reason do poor people line up to see the sultan?

2. What is the risk these people take in wanting to see the sultan?

3. What words does Ibn Battuta use to show that people might fear Muhammad bin Tughluq?

4. What positive qualities of Muhammad bin Tughluq does Ibn Battuta describe?

CHAPTER TEST 8

THE ASIAN WORLD, 600–1500

NAME _____ DATE _____

A. MULTIPLE CHOICE

Circle the letter of the best answer for each question.

1. Which of the following rulers was born a slave?
   a. Qutb-ud-din Aybak   c. Ala-ud-din
   b. Raziya   d. Muhammad bi Tughluq

2. Why did Aybak order the destruction of 27 Hindu temples in Delhi?
   a. In order to anger the local population.
   b. He needed the stones and bricks to build his mosques.
   c. The temples were filled with religious statues, which were prohibited by his religion, Islam.
   d. He wanted to get the Hindus to pay a special tax.

3. All of the following are true of Raziya **except**
   a. she dressed and acted like a man.
   b. everyone thought she was a great leader.
   c. she was captured by her political enemies and married one of her captors.
   d. she forced the ruler of Bengal to surrender to her.

4. Under Ala-ud-din's leadership
   a. the sultanate's territory was reduced.
   b. no Hindu temples were looted.
   c. the country's economy suffered.
   d. India became the premier source for colorful cotton textiles.

5. What did Timur Leng hope to do with the treasure he acquired in India?
   a. fund an invasion of China
   b. help the Hindus
   c. protect the Muslims of Delhi
   d. weaken the Delhi sultanate

B. SHORT ANSWER

Answer these questions in two or three sentences.

6. What changes did Aybak, the first sultan, bring about when he introduced Islam to Delhi?
   _____
   _____

7. Identify and describe the first woman sultan, and tell what happened to her.
   _____
   _____

C. ESSAY

On a separate sheet of paper, describe the ways that Hindu and Muslim cultures influenced each other in India.

CHAPTER 9

KHAN AND EMPEROR: THE YUAN DYNASTY IN CHINA
PAGES 113–123

FOR HOMEWORK

STUDENT STUDY GUIDE

pages 43–46

CAST OF CHARACTERS

Marco Polo Italian traveler to China

Khubilai Khan (KOO-buh-lie kahn) grandson of Genghis Khan who became Great Khan and later founded Yuan dynasty of China

Liu Bingzhong (lyoh bing-joong) Chinese scholar and adviser to Khubilai Khan

Guo Shoujing (gwoh show-jing) Chinese mathematician, astronomer, engineer and adviser to Khubilai Khan

Zhao Mengfu (jao mung-foo) Chinese artist and scholar-official under Yuan dynasty

CHAPTER SUMMARY

Marco Polo and his father and uncle arrived in China during the Yuan Dynasty. At this time, Khubilai Khan brought China under the rule of the Mongols. He reorganized the country into ethnic groups and made governmental reforms to keep the Mongols in power. He respected different religious beliefs as equally valid paths to god. Khubilai brought Korea under Chinese rule but was not able to conquer Japan or Southeast Asia.

PERFORMANCE OBJECTIVES

▶ To identify Khubilai Khan as an important figure in Chinese history
▶ To describe the rise of the Mongol Empire
▶ To understand the importance of the developments made during the rule of Khubilai Khan
▶ To analyze Khubilai Khan's style of ruling

BUILDING BACKGROUND

Write *United States* on the board and ask students why they think the country's founders chose this name. Have them give examples from U.S. history that would explain why the idea of unity of the states would be important. Explain that Khubilai Khan also had to think of the meaning for the name of his dynasty and chose Yuan which means "origin" or "primary." Ask students to suggest possible reasons for Khubilai's choice of Yuan as the name of his dynasty.

VOCABULARY

dynasty a long succession of rulers from the same family
tributary a stream feeding a larger stream or lake; also a state that pays allegiance to another state
cavalry an army on horseback

WORKING WITH PRIMARY SOURCES

During the reign of Khubilai Khan, a new north-south canal system was built, making it possible to transport goods to transport rice and other goods from all over the country to the capital. The canal made it easier for everyone, including visitors and merchants to travel around China. One such traveler, Marco Polo, claimed to have visited China by way of the Silk Road, a route by which silk and other items had long traveled from China to Europe. To give students a sense of what it was like for European merchants to travel in China in the 13th and 14th centuries, go to Francesco di Balducci Pegolotti's *Guide for Merchants* in The *Medieval & Early Modern World Primary Sources and Reference Volume* (see page 62). This merchant from Florence wrote advice for Europeans traveling east through Asia and to China.

74   CHAPTER 9

READING COMPREHENSION QUESTIONS

1. Why did Khubilai Khan like the name *Yuan* for his dynasty? (*Yuan means "origin" or "primary," which to him symbolized the return to a golden age of good and simple government.*)
2. What were the four ethnic and geographic groups that Khubilai Khan divided China into? (*Mongol warriors; people of central and West Asian heritage, such as Turks, Muslims, Tibetans, Persians, and Europeans; "people of Han" from Northern China, including Chinese, Khitans, Jurchens, and Koreans; and the Nanren, who were the southerners.*)
3. How did the Grand Canal change life in China? (*The canal made it possible to transport rice and other goods from the southern provinces of China to the new capital at Dadu. It greatly improved the transportation network of northern China.*)
4. Why did Khubilai Khan dispatch troops to Japan? (*The Japanese regent did not respond to Khubilai's missions or recognize the Yuan government.*)
5. Why did many people resent the rulers after Renzong? (*These Mongol rulers held the highest position, kept themselves separate from the (Han) Chinese, and discouraged intermarriage between Mongols and Han.*)

CRITICAL THINKING QUESTIONS

1. What effect do you think Khubilai Khan's tolerance for different religious beliefs had on the people of China? (*Possible answer: People felt safe to worship and pray as they wished. They did not fear that they would be killed or punished for their beliefs.*)
2. Did Khubilai Khan's successors continue with his same methods of ruling? Explain. (*No, Khubilai sent out many military expeditions during his reign, whereas Chengzong reduced the amount spent on the military. Khubilai ruled mainly through the Mongol military, but Renzong reinstituted the examination system to employ Chinese scholar-officials.*)

SOCIAL SCIENCES

Economics The Grand Canal of China is the longest canal in the world. Building the canal had an enormous impact on China's economy and society. Have students do research on the Internet or in the encyclopedia to find out more about the economic impact the building of the Grand Canal had on China. One helpful website is *http://library.thinkquest.org/20443/grandcanal.html*.

READING AND LANGUAGE ARTS

Reading Nonfiction Ask students to preview the chapter, paying close attention to the features, such as pictures, headings, and sidebars. Ask them to make a two-column chart. In the first column, students can list any questions they may have about the content of the chapter such as, *Why are the people in these pictures important? What is meant by the heading "Keeping an Open Mind"?* Then students can write answers to their questions in the second column as they read the chapter.

THEN and NOW

During the time of Khubilai Khan, the Mongolian Empire included China, where the Mongols became the ruling class. Today, there are about 5 million Mongols, many of whom live in the country of Mongolia, and others of whom live in China. For more information see the website *www.nomadicjourneys.com/mongolia/culheritage.asp*.

LINKING DISCIPLINES

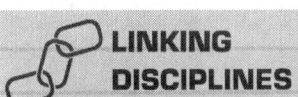

Science A canal is a waterway that is built by people. Have students investigate what a canal does and how a canal is built. Students can research the Grand Canal in China or other canals including the Suez Canal, the Panama Canal, and the Erie Canal.

THE ASIAN WORLD, 600–1500

LITERATURE CONNECTION

Wilson, Diane L. *I Rode a Horse of Milk White Jade.* HarperTrophy, 1999. In early fourteenth-century China, Oyuna tells her granddaughter of her girlhood in Mongolia and how love for her horse enabled her to win an important race and bring good luck to her family.

Holland, Cecelia. *Ghost on the Steppe.* Atheneum, 1969. Djela of Mongolia is banished to a northern station to herd cattle and horses for telling his father a lie but it is in performing this penance that he glimpses himself as heir to a tradition and a way of life.

LITERACY TIPS

In addition to using the suggestions in the Supporting Learning and Extending Learning sections, refer back frequently to pages 16–19 for strategies and advice from a literacy coach.

Using Language Have students look in the chapter for hyphenated adjectives. Explain that some of these adjectives are hyphenated because they are actually non-adjectives, such as nouns and verbs, that are being used as adjectives to describe a noun. For example, in *porcelain-producing center*, "porcelain-producing" is actually a noun. The words are hyphenated to show that they are describing the center where the porcelain producing takes place. Students may also notice that in these hyphenated describing words, the first word describes the second. For example, *porcelain* describes the type of *producing*. Have students look for the other hyphenated adjectives in the chapter and explain their meanings in a similar way. Some examples include: best-governed, well-educated, labor-service, and upper-class.

WRITING

Interview Ask students to imagine they are reporters assigned to interview Khubilai Khan about his plans for China. Have them write *who, what, when, where, why,* and *how* questions they would like to ask him. Then using what they have learned from the chapter, have students write the answers they think Khubilai Khan might give.

SUPPORTING LEARNING

English Language Learners Have students reread the paragraph with the heading "Keeping an Open Mind," about the various religious groups in China at the time of Khubilai Khan. Students can ask members of their families about the religions practiced in their countries of origin. Then have students write a short paragraph explaining one or more of these religions.

Struggling Readers Students can work in small groups to discuss the accomplishments in China during the rule of Kubilai Khan. They can use the main idea map to organize their ideas (see reproducibles at the back of this guide). In the center circle, they can write *Accomplishments during Kubilai Khan's rule*. In the outer circles, they can write information about what Kubilai Khan did. Invite students to add more circles to the map if necessary.

EXTENDING LEARNING

Enrichment According to the chapter, Marco Polo would not have been able to have an official career in China if it were not for Khubilai Khan. Have students research what Marco Polo was able to see and do during the seventeen years he spent in China. One helpful website is www.silk-road.com/artl/marcopolo.shtml. Then have students present what they found in their research. (Some experts doubt that Marco Polo went to China at all. As an extra challenge, invite students to investigate the evidence and present their findings to the class.)

Extension Invite a volunteer to read aloud the paragraphs that describe the four groups into which Khubilai Khan organized the people of China. Then organize students into small groups and have each group discuss what it might have been like to be a member of a particular group in China. Then have the groups share their ideas with each other.

THE WORLD OF KHUBILAI KHAN, 1260–1294

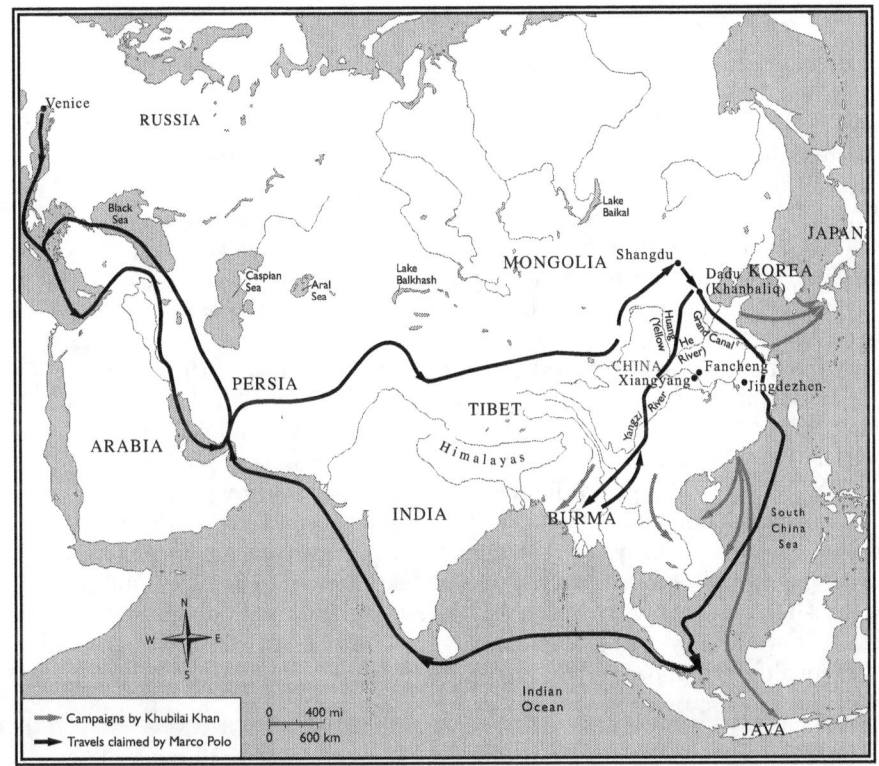

Directions

Study the map and then answer the questions that follow.

1. What cities did Marco Polo claim to have visited? Include the city from which he began his travels.

2. Identify the two new Chinese capitals designed and built by Khubilai Khan after he came to power. Explain why he built two capitals instead of just one.

3. What modern Chinese city is located near the site of one of Khubilai's capital cities?

4. What feature greatly improved the transport of goods to the new capital at Dadu? Circle this feature on the map and write on the map how it was used.

5. What large bodies of water did Marco Polo travel through on his voyage to and from China? Label any that aren't already labeled on the map.

CHAPTER 9 BLM — THE ASIAN WORLD, 600–1500

NAME _____ DATE _____

PRIMARY SOURCES

Directions

Read this excerpt from Marco Polo's book, *Travels*. Then answer the questions.

> From the city of Khanbalig [Dadu, now Beijing] there are many roads leading to different provinces, and upon each of these . . . at the distance of twenty-five or thirty miles . . . here are stations . . . called *yamb* or post-houses. At each station four hundred good horses are kept in constant readiness, in order that all messengers going and coming on the business of the grand khan . . . may have relays, and, leaving their tired horses, be supplied with fresh ones. . . . The royal messengers go and return through every province and kingdom of the empire with the greatest convenience and ease, in which the grand khan exhibits a superiority over every other emperor, king, or human being. . . .
>
> When it is necessary that the messengers should proceed with extraordinary speed as in the cases of giving information of a disturbance in any part of the country, the rebellion of a chief, or other important matters, they ride two hundred, or sometimes two hundred and fifty miles in the course of a day. On such occasions they carry with them a tablet having on it a picture of a falcon, as a signal of the urgency of their business, . . . and they wrap their bodies tightly [with cloth bandages, for support,] bind a cloth around their heads, and push their horses to the greatest speed. . . . Changing in the same manner at every stage, until the day closes, they perform a journey of two hundred and fifty miles. They continue thus until they come to the next post-house at twenty-five miles distance, where they find . . . other horses fresh and in a state to work; they spring upon them without taking any rest, and continue. . . . Messengers qualified to undergo this extraordinary degree of fatigue are held in high estimation.

1. How did this system of sending messages benefit the Grand Khan?

_____
_____

2. How does the system of sending messages that Marco Polo described compare with the method used in 19th-century America? With the system we use today?

_____
_____
_____
_____
_____

CHAPTER TEST 9

THE ASIAN WORLD, 600–1500

NAME _____ DATE _____

A. MULTIPLE CHOICE

Circle the letter of the best answer for each question.

1. The Grand Canal was important because
   a. rice and other goods could be transported out of the capital.
   b. it was easy to build.
   c. it separated the other waterways of China.
   d. it greatly improved the transportation network of northern China.

2. How did Khubilai Khan keep the Mongols and their supporters permanently in power?
   a. He appointed many non-Chinese to important posts.
   b. He began an examination system.
   c. He appointed the Nanren people to government offices.
   d. He appointed the "people of Han" to military positions.

3. Which best describes Khubilai Khan's relationship with Korea?
   a. The Koreans did not accept Khubilai Khan as superior to the king.
   b. Khubilai Khan controlled Korea very closely and made many demands on the Koreans.
   c. Koreans would not sign a peace treaty with Khubilai Khan.
   d. Khubilai Khan was not protective of the Korean interests.

4. Which are the two countries Khubilai Khan could not get under Mongol control?
   a. China and Korea
   b. Korea and Burma
   c. Burma and Japan
   d. Japan and China

B. SHORT ANSWER

Answer these questions in two or three sentences.

5. What developments took place in China under the leadership of Khubilai Khan?
   _____
   _____
   _____

6. What factors eventually weakened the Mongol dynasty after Renzong?
   _____
   _____
   _____

C. ESSAY

Read the popular anti-government ballad of the Yuan dynasty below.
> Thieves get to be official and officials behave like thieves,
> The good can't be told from the bad, alas, how sad!

On a separate piece of paper, explain what this quotation means. Then write an essay explaining how this quotation applies to the reign of Khubilai Khan.

CHAPTER 10
WARRIORS RULE: KAMAKURA AND ASHIKAGA JAPAN
PAGES 124–135

STUDENT STUDY GUIDE

pages 47–50

CAST OF CHARACTERS

Shinran (shin-rahn) influential Japanese Buddhist priest of Pure Land school

Nichiren (nee-chee-ren) founder of militant Lotus Sutra sect of Japanese Buddhism

Godaigo (go-DIE-go) Japanese emperor who tried to restore power to the throne

Ashikaga Takauji (ah-shee-kAH-gah) founder of Ashikaga shogunate

Muso Soseki (moo-SOH soh-seh-kee) Japanese Zen master

CHAPTER SUMMARY

Between 1185 and 1500, leadership of Japan changed from one of imperial government to military rule. After the Minamoto clan wiped out the Taira forces, weak leadership led the Hojo clan to seize power. During this time, new forms of Buddhism, the Pure Land, Nichiren and Zen sects became popular. Japan resumed diplomatic relations with China and absorbed many new Chinese cultural influences.

PERFORMANCE OBJECTIVES

▶ To explain the transition of power in Japan from one clan to another
▶ To explain the rise of the shogun leadership in Japan
▶ To understand the rise of Buddhist sects in Japan
▶ To describe the impact of relations between Japan and China on Japanese culture

BUILDING BACKGROUND

Ask students to think about the types of art they think of when they think of particular religions. They may mention that Muslim mosques often have ornate designs and tilework in them. Catholic churches have paintings and sculptures. Explain that in this chapter, students will read about different types of arts that were inspired by Zen Buddhism.

VOCABULARY

disciples followers
exiled banished from one's home country, usually a punishment for a crime
meditation deep thought and reflection
abdicate to formally give up the throne or power

WORKING WITH PRIMARY SOURCES

When the Buddhist teacher Nichiren was exiled to a small island in the Sea of Japan, he wrote, "Birds cry but shed no tears: Nichiren does not cry, but his tears are never dry." Have students discuss the meaning of this statement. Ask questions such as: *How is Nichiren feeling? How does he think he is like or unlike the birds?*

GEOGRAPHY CONNECTION

Location Have students study the map on page 126 of the Student Edition. Introduce Japan as a nation of islands, and ask what this geographical fact might mean about Japan's history. Ask students which events in the chapter were directly affected by the fact that Japan is surrounded by ocean on all sides. Examples include the clash between the Taira and the Minamoto clan, which resulted in a naval battle in the western Inland Sea (locate this event on the map), in which the seven-year-old emperor was drowned. Explain that Japan's island geography also makes it more subject to extreme weather from the oceans. Ask students what effect weather might have had in turning back foreign invasions. For an example, talk about the Mongol invasions in 1274 and 1281, both of which failed in part because of rough storms from the sea.

READING COMPREHENSION QUESTIONS

1. Were Taira Kiyomori's expectations for the future of Japan met? Explain. (*No, Kiyomori expected his heirs to rule Japan for many generations, but the Minamoto wiped out the Tiara forces. When the situation looked hopeless for the Tiara, a noblewoman drowned Kiyomori's grandson, the only heir, to keep him from falling into the hands of the enemy. This ended the possibility of Kiyomori's family's continued rule.*)

2. What was the goal of the shogun government? (*to establish and perpetuate the power of the military class at the expense of the old Heian aristocracy*)

3. How did the Hojo clan come to rule Japan? (*Yoritomo's sons were weak rulers, so the family of Yoritomo's wife seized power. They established a regency for Minamoto shoguns and thereby dominated the government.*)

4. How did Nichiren gain a large following for the Lotus sutra form of Buddhism? (*He was a charismatic speaker with a strong sense of personal mission. Nichiren predicted that Japan would be attacked by the Mongols as punishment to the Hojo rulers for their support of the other Buddhist schools. When the Mongols attacked, many people chose to follow Nichiren.*)

5. How did relations between Japan and China influence Japan? (*Japanese commerce improved through trade and new ideas about the Zen arts began to show up in Japanese culture.*)

CRITICAL THINKING QUESTIONS

1. How did Yoritomo use the *bakufu*, or tent government, he established to consolidate his power? (*He made it appear that he was always on a military campaign to defend the emperor. The emperors of Japan were only figureheads of government, with no real power. So by becoming shogun and ruling on behalf of the emperor, Yoritomo would become the one truly powerful ruler of all Japan.*)

2. Why did the Hojo regency feel threatened by Nichiren? (*Possible answer: After Nichiren correctly predicted the attack by the Mongols and increased his following, the Hojo regency feared that Nichiren would gather his followers and turn them against the government.*)

SOCIAL SCIENCES

Civics The chapter discusses two Buddhist leaders who were exiled by the government for their ideas, lifestyles, or outspoken attitudes about the government. Have students work in pairs to research other people in history who have been exiled for their beliefs or actions (for example, Roger Williams or Anne Hutchinson in colonial America). Then have the pairs present their findings to the class.

THEN and NOW

The military aristocracy was interested in Zen ideas, specifically the discipline of meditation. Today, people all over the world use meditation as a way to relax, relieve stress and depression, and feel more centered.

LINKING DISCIPLINES

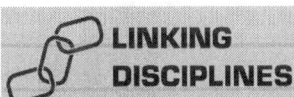

Science The kamikaze, or divine winds, that forced the Mongol armies to return to China were typhoons. These typhoons, which occur in the Pacific Ocean, are similar to the hurricanes of the Atlantic Ocean. Have students do research on the causes of typhoons and their impact on people.

LITERATURE CONNECTION

Inoue, Yasushi. *Lou-Lan and Other Stories*. Kodansha America, 1994. This book consists of six stories about the hidden treasures of Asia's past. Tales of historical fiction, they are also extremely well-researched forays into remote geographical areas and little-known periods of history. Inoue is the author of several other works of fiction available in translation, including *Tan-huang*, another historical novel.

LITERACY TIPS

In addition to using the suggestions in the Supporting Learning and Extending Learning sections, refer back frequently to pages 16–19 for strategies and advice from a literacy coach.

READING AND LANGUAGE ARTS

Reading Nonfiction Students can create a sequence of events chart showing how one situation led to the next in the changing of power in Japan. The chart should include the names of important people and the actions that led to the changes.

Using Language Ask students to skim the chapter looking for words in italics. Ask them to share their ideas about why these words are italicized. If necessary, elicit that these are all Japanese words. Point out that these words appear in italics followed by their meanings in regular type. Have students work with a partner to make a list of these words and their meanings in their history journals.

WRITING

Journal While Nichiren was in exile, he wrote to his followers. Perhaps he also kept a journal. Discuss with students what Nichiren's experience in exile might have been like. Then have students write a journal entry from Nichiren's perspective telling about his time in exile.

SUPPORTING LEARNING

English Language Learners The chapter is filled with descriptive language. Help students recognize that adjectives are describing words. Adjectives describe nouns and, in written text, are often located just before nouns. Ask students to work in pairs to make a list of at least 15 adjectives and the nouns they describe. Then have students use the adjectives in sentences using a new noun.

Struggling Readers Have students use the T-chart (see reproducibles at the back of this guide) to show the actions of the people in the chapter and the effects those actions caused. Then have students work in small groups to compare their charts. Encourage them to notice when an effect on one person's chart is a cause on another person's chart.

EXTENDING LEARNING

Enrichment The Zen arts continue to be an important part of Japanese culture. Have students choose one of the types of arts mentioned in the chapter, such as architecture, raising bonsai trees, painting, swordsmanship, or the Noh theater, and research how the Japanese study these art forms. Students can answer questions, such as: *What type of training is required? Who participates?* Students can then present what they have learned to small groups.

Extension Have students work in small groups to learn about the Japanese tea ceremony. Then have them act out the steps of the tea ceremony.

PRIMARY SOURCES

Directions

Read the poem by Zen Buddhist master Muso Soseki. Then answer the questions.

> When there is nowhere
> That you have determined
> To call your own,
> then no matter where you go
> You are always going home.

1. What is the meaning of this poem?

2. How does this poem reflect the ideas of Zen Buddhism?

3. Write your own poem on a similar theme.

PRIMARY SOURCES

Directions

Read the excerpt from Yoshida Kenko. Then answer the questions.

> There is a charm about a neat and proper dwelling house, although this world, 'tis true, is but a temporary abode. Even the moonlight, when it strikes into the house where a good man lives in peaceful ease, seem to gain in friendly brilliancy.
>
> The man is to be envied who lives in a house, not of the modern, garish [tacky] kind, but set among venerable trees, with a garden where plants grow wild and yet seem to have been disposed with care, verandas and fences tastefully arranged, and all its furnishings simple but antique.
>
> A house which multitudes of workmen have devoted all their ingenuity to decorate, where rare and strange things from home and abroad are set out in array, and where event he trees and shrubs are trained unnaturally—such is an unpleasant sight, depressing to look at, to say nothing of spending one's days therein. Nor, gazing on it, can one but reflect how easily it might vanish in a moment of time.
>
> The appearance of a house is in some sort of an index to the character of its occupant.

1. When does the moonlight look brilliant?
_____

Kenko states that:
 "The appearance of a house is in some sort an index to the character of its occupant."

2. What type of person might Kenko think lives in the first house he describes?
_____
_____

3. What type of person might he say lives in the second house he describes?
_____
_____

4. Write a short paragraph describing the type of home that Kenko would like to live in.
_____
_____
_____
_____

CHAPTER TEST 10

THE ASIAN WORLD, 600–1500

NAME _____ **DATE** _____

A. MULTIPLE CHOICE

Circle the letter of the best answer for each question.

1. How did the Hojo clan come to power?
   a. They seized power from the sons of Yoritomo.
   b. They drowned the seven-year-old emperor, Antoku.
   c. They fought against the Minamoto shoguns.
   d. They found many followers through their support of the Lotus Sutra form of Buddhism.

2. Which best describes Yoritomo's form of government?
   a. government under the all-powerful leadership of the emperor
   b. leadership by a family
   c. a system of child emperors and regents
   d. a military system run by the shogun

3. How did Yoritomo take control of the government of Japan?
   a. He removed the emperor from the throne and took over.
   b. He established a separate government, backed by the military, apart from the capital.
   c. He launched a revolution.
   d. He inherited the throne.

4. How were relations with China re-established?
   a. The Mongols came to Japan.
   b. China gave money to Japan to pay the expenses of the military government.
   c. Godaigo sent an official mission to China.
   d. China sent gift of silk and porcelain to Japan.

5. Which of the following practices is **not** associated with the Zen sect of Buddhism?
   a. intensive study of scriptures
   b. raising bonsai trees
   c. creating gardens of stones and raked gravel
   d. painting skills

B. SHORT ANSWER

Answer these questions in two or three sentences.

6. What led to the exile of Nichiren?

   _____
   _____
   _____
   _____

7. Explain the appeal of Zen Buddhism to Japan's military class.

   _____
   _____

C. ESSAY

On a separate piece of paper, write a few paragraphs to answer the question.

How did Japan benefit from its new relationship with China?

CHAPTER 11

FRESH DAWN: KORYO AND EARLY CHOSON KOREA
PAGES 136–147

STUDENT STUDY GUIDE

pages 51–54

CAST OF CHARACTERS

Yi Songgye (ee sohng-gyeh) also known as King T'aejo (Tie-joh), general and founder of Korea's Choson dynasty

Wang Kon (wong kun) founder of Koryo dynasty in Korea

Wonjong (wun jahng) Korean king of Koryo dynasty who established close relations with Mongols

Sejong (SEH-johng) third king of Choson dynasty who was considered Korea's greatest king

Munjong (MUHN-johng) fourth king of Korea's Choson dynasty who sponsored historical scholarship

CHAPTER SUMMARY

The rulers of Korea between 1388 and 1453 brought the country to the forefront in invention and education. Although Korea came under the rule of the Mongols in 1273, the country continued its progress. Korea's relations with China allowed the country to improve in the areas of trade and intellectual development.

PERFORMANCE OBJECTIVES

▶ To identify the leaders of Korea between 1388 and 1453
▶ To understand the relationship between Korea and China, as well as China's impact on the development of Korean ideas
▶ To describe the lasting accomplishments of the Korean leaders between 1388 and 1453

BUILDING BACKGROUND

Ask students to share what they think of when they hear the words *fresh dawn*. Have students write their thoughts in their history journals. Explain that these words are the translation of Choson, the ancient Chinese name for Korea. Invite students, as they read, to write any other ideas they have about whether this name is appropriate for Korea during this time.

VOCABULARY

aristocratic of a privileged rank

besieged bombarded; or under attack by being completely surrounded and cut off from supplies

unprecedented never before known or experienced

WORKING WITH PRIMARY SOURCES

The leaders described in the chapter had innovative ideas and brought Korea to the forefront in education and invention. In *The Medieval & Early Modern World Primary Sources and Reference Volume*, see the edict from King Munjong in 1451 (page 65). Read this passage to students and have them discuss what type of leader they think Munjong was. Elicit answers by asking questions such as: *How does Munjong feel about the people he leads? Is Munjong an innovative thinker? Why or why not?*

GEOGRAPHY CONNECTION

Location Have students study the map of Korea on page 139 and then flip to the map on pages 12-13 to see Korea in the context of Asia. Point out the fact that Korea is a peninsula, and ask students to define this term. Ask students if they know of any other peninsulas on the world map, for example Italy, Florida, Arabia. What do these areas all have in common? Have them consider why being a peninsula is a significant fact for Korea (as a region surrounded on three sides with water, it has its own natural borders; even though it was ruled by the Mongols, it still retained a separate cultural identity).

CHAPTER 11

READING COMPREHENSION QUESTIONS

1. What was the difficult decision General Yi Songgye faced in 1388? (*He had to decide whether or not to follow the king's orders and attack China even though he knew that his army could never win against China.*)
2. Why did the Mongols launch a full-scale attack on Korea in 1231? (*The Mongols were angry because the Koreans killed a Mongol ambassador to Korea.*)
3. Why was King Sejong considered one of the most accomplished and enlightened monarchs in history? (*He was responsible for the establishment of a research institute, the founding of an academy of Confucian studies, and the development of a Korean system of writing. During his reign, Koreans invented bronze instruments that improved the accuracy of astronomers' observations, an accurate rain gauge, and a water-clock that kept accurate time.*)

CRITICAL THINKING QUESTIONS

1. To what did General Yi owe his success? Did some Koreans at the time have other ideas about why he was successful? (*General Yi succeeded because he was an experienced military commander, a natural leader, and was willing to take risks when necessary. But many Koreans thought that he must have succeeded because he had good ancestors.*)
2. What do you think was the most important invention or contribution made by the Koreans during the period discussed in the chapter? Explain. (*Answers will vary.*)

SOCIAL SCIENCES

Science, Technology, and Society Have students work in pairs to research the development of one of the inventions mentioned in the chapter. Ask them to find out how this invention affected the people of the time and/or how this invention has evolved into a machine or tool we use today. Then have the pairs present what they learned to the class.

READING AND LANGUAGE ARTS

Reading Nonfiction On page 141, the text discusses the accomplishments of King Taejong. Have students read this paragraph and pick out the main idea and list the details used to support it.

Using Language Point out that the chapter contains many adverbs. Explain that adverbs are used to describe how an action, a verb, is done. Point out that adverbs often, but not always, end in -*ly* and that sometimes a noun may appear between the verb and the adverb as in "write Korean phonetically." Have students work in pairs to find at least five adverbs, and the verbs they describe in the chapter and write them in their history journals. Then students can use these adverbs to write their own sentences using new verbs.

WRITING

Persuasion Ask students to imagine that they are scholars working with King Sejong. They need to convince the people of Korea to use the new Korean writing system they have developed. Have them write a letter to the people in which they try to convince them to see the benefits of the new writing system.

THEN and NOW

The leaders of Korea discussed in the chapter encouraged the development of new ideas and inventions. In the United States today, it is common for the government to fund programs for the development of new ideas and inventions such as space travel and more efficient energy systems.

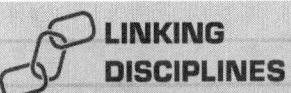 LINKING DISCIPLINES

Health Under the rule of King Sejong, medical scholars produced a manual that included 1,500 different acupuncture techniques. Have students research the process and uses of acupuncture and determine whether they see benefits in this technique.

THE ASIAN WORLD, 600–1500

LITERATURE CONNECTION

Korean literature is not as readily available as that of China or Japan. However, you might wish to consult:

Lee, Peter H., ed. *Anthology of Korean Literature: From Early Times to the Nineteenth Century.* University Press of Hawaii, 1980. This collection is included in the UNESCO collection of representative works.

Additionally, this website offers information on the history and different parts of Korean literature, as well as other resources on the overall body of works: www.asianinfo.org/asianinfo/korea/literature.htm

LITERACY TIPS

In addition to using the suggestions in the Supporting Learning and Extending Learning sections, refer back frequently to pages 16–19 for strategies and advice from a literacy coach.

SUPPORTING LEARNING

English Language Learners With students, read the quotation from King Sejong on page 145 regarding the need for the Korean language to have its own letters rather than using those of the Chinese language. Have students discuss how their first languages are written. Do they use the same characters as in English? Do the characters have the same sounds as in English? Do the characters represent sounds or whole words or ideas? Ask volunteers who know different languages to each write the same sentence in the language of their country of origin. Then have students compare the characters and sounds of the language. They may or may not find similarity between these languages and English.

Struggling Readers Have students work in pairs to use the outline graphic organizer (see reproducibles at the back of this guide) to keep track of the information in the chapter. One student can write a main idea and the other student can write a supporting detail.

EXTENDING LEARNING

Enrichment King Taejo established close relations with Ming China, even to the point of adopting the Ming calendar. Have students work in pairs to research the Ming calendar and compare it with the calendar we use today.

Extension Have students work in small groups to create a diagram of the water-clock developed during the reign of King Sejong based on the description in the chapter. Then have the groups present their diagrams to the class.

KINGDOM OF CHOSON, 1419–1450

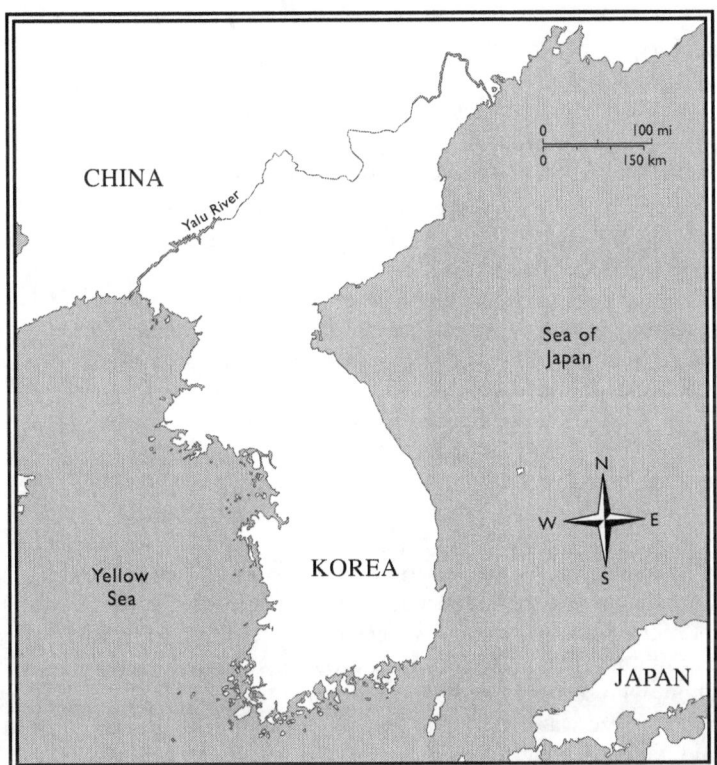

Directions

Make the following changes to the map below to show Choson during King Sejong's reign. Then answer the following questions.

1. Indicate on the map with shading or a pattern the boundaries of Choson from 1419 to 1450.

2. Key this shading in the legend.

3. Locate and label the cities of Kaesong and Hanyang.

4. Put a circle around the label of the city that had been the capital before the Choson dynasty. Put a square around the label of the city that Choson king T'aejo made the new capital after he accepted the throne in 1392.

5. Why did the Choson king change the capital?

_____

_____

PRIMARY SOURCES

Directions

Read the passage from the *History of the Koryo Dynasty*.

In King Sinjong's first year [1198], the private slave Manjok and six others, while collecting firewood on a northern mountain, gathered public and private slaves and plotted, saying, "Since the coup [seizure of power] in the year [1170] and the countercoup in the year [1173], the country has witnessed many high officials rising from slave status. How could these generals and ministers be different from us in origin? If one has an opportunity, anybody can make it. Why should we still toil and suffer under the whip?"

The slaves all agreed with this. They cut several thousand pieces of yellow paper and wrote the character *chong* [adult man] on each one as their symbol. They pledged: "We will start from the hallways of Hungguk Monastery and go to the polo grounds. Once all are assembled and start to beat drums and yell, the eunuchs [neutered male palace servants] in the palace will certainly respond. The public slaves will take control of the palace by force, and we will stage an uprising inside the capital, first killing Ch'oe Ch'unghon [the general who had suppressed rebellions in 1196] and others. If each slave will kill his master and burn the slave registers, there will be no people of humble status in the country, and we can all become nobles, generals, and ministers."

On the date set to meet, their numbers did not exceed several hundred, so they feared they would not succeed and changed their plans, promising to meet at Poje Temple this time. All were ordered: "If the affair is not kept secret, then we will not succeed. Be careful not to reveal it." Sunjong, the slave of Doctor of Legal Studies Han Ch'ungyu, reported this incident to his master. Ch'ungyu told Ch'oe Ch'unghon, who seized Manjok and more than one hundred others and threw them into the river. Ch'ungyu was promoted to warder [watchman] in the Royal Archives, and Sunjong was granted eighty *yang* [one *yang* = 1.325 ounces] of white gold and freed and upgraded to commoner status. Since the remaining gang members could not all be executed, the king decreed that the matter be dropped.

Write an essay explaining how the lives of the people in this passage compare with the lives of the people during the Choson dynasty.

CHAPTER TEST 11

THE ASIAN WORLD, 600–1500

NAME _____ DATE _____

A. MULTIPLE CHOICE

Circle the letter of the best answer for each question.

1. Why did General Yi Songgye refuse to attack China?
    a. The Korean kingdom of Koryo was still loyal to the Mongol rulers.
    b. He wanted to do what the Korean king asked him to do.
    c. He was too busy fighting against Japanese pirates.
    d. He did not think his army could win.

2. Which invention was the result of encouragement by King T'aejong?
    a. moveable metal-type printing
    b. the water-clock
    c. the science of acupuncture
    d. the rain gauge

3. All of the following were begun under the rule of King Sejong **except**
    a. the Hall of Worthies.
    b. the Hall for Illustrating the Cardinal Principles.
    c. the compilation of a History of Korea.
    d. the use of the rain gauge to predict yields of important crops.

4. What was notable about the Choson dynasty?
    a. It lasted until 1450.
    b. It was one of the most accomplished and peaceful dynasties in human history.
    c. Fewer reforms were proposed than in other dynasties.
    d. The Yi family was unable to retain control of the throne.

B. SHORT ANSWER

Answer these questions in two or three sentences.

5. Describe the sequence of events, beginning with the founding of Koryo, that led to Sejong becoming king of Korea.

   _____
   _____
   _____

6. How did the Koryo government benefit from the Mongol peace?

   _____
   _____
   _____

C. ESSAY

On a separate sheet of paper, discuss the influences China had on Korea.

CHAPTER 12
RISE AND SHINE: RULERS AND TREASURE SHIPS IN MING CHINA PAGES 148–160

FOR HOMEWORK

STUDENT STUDY GUIDE

pages 55–58

CAST OF CHARACTERS

Zhu Yuanzhang (joo yooann-jahng), also known as Ming Taizu (ming TIE-dzoo) founder of Ming dynasty

Zhu Di (joo dee) also known as Yongle (yuhngluh) second emperor of Ming dynasty who sponsored "treasure fleet" voyages

Zheng He (jeng huh) eunuch admiral who led Ming "treasure fleet" voyages

CHAPTER SUMMARY

Zhu Yuanzhang (Ming Taizu) was a commoner rebel who rose up to found the Ming ("Bright") Dynasty in China. Under his leadership, the education system was reformed to serve the people. Taizu imposed harsh punishments on those he thought had done wrong. Zhu Di, also known as Yongle, became the next Ming leader. Under his rule, China undertook maritime trade and expeditions and became the richest country in the world. After rising and shining in these ways, the Ming adopted a defensive policy toward the rest of the world and devoted itself to developing China's internal welfare.

PERFORMANCE OBJECTIVES

- To understand the rise of the Ming Dynasty
- To identify the rulers of the Ming Dynasty
- To describe a quest for military expansion in the early Ming followed by an emphasis on peace and agricultural prosperity later on

BUILDING BACKGROUND

Ask students to share what they know about trade by sea. Discuss some of the products that might be traded between countries by ships. Which United States cities may be centers for this type of trade? Explain that in this chapter students will read about the increase in—but also limitations on—Ming involvement in maritime trade.

VOCABULARY

epidemic an outbreak of a disease that spreads rapidly

retaliation revenge

regulation a rule or order issued by an agency of the government

prosperous successful

WORKING WITH PRIMARY SOURCES

After Emperor Yongle died, China became less of a military force. Read the joke by the Ming humorist, Feng Menglong, in the Student Edition (page 160), and discuss the meaning with students. Ask why the students do or do not find this joke amusing and discuss how this joke represents a general idea about the leadership of China towards the end of the Ming.

GEOGRAPHY CONNECTION

Interaction The Ming period in the history of China had two opposing directions: One was to connect and trade with other nations, the other was to withdraw and secure the empire's border. Have students compare the map on page 156 with the map on pages 14–15. Ask if students think China was dependent on trade for survival (*no, because of its natural resources, particularly the rice-producing provinces in the south, although merchants prospered from trading on the Silk Road*). Point out to students that the Silk Road lost its importance in the early 15th century, because the Ming could never fully gain control over the steppe and the western region of Central Asia. Meanwhile, Mongols from the north were a constant threat, making it necessary to concentrate efforts to expand and reinforce the Great Wall. Discuss the factors that might make a large state like China be more concerned with securing its borders than invading or conquering neighboring states (*China was so large that protecting it from outside invasions was already a big task; also invading other states meant acquiring more land the government would have to defend.*)

READING COMPREHENSION QUESTIONS

1. Why did people begin to question the Yuan Dynasty's right to rule? (*There had been floods, droughts, disease, and famine in the country, which led people to believe that the Yuan Dynasty was no longer favored by heaven to rule.*)

2. What led Zhu Yuanzhang to become the founder and leader of the Ming Dynasty? (*Although beginning life as a beggar, he became a strong military leader whose army took the wealthy cities of the Yangzi Valley. These victories gave him the confidence he needed to become founder and leader of the Ming Dynasty.*)

3. How did Yongle minimize conflict with the Mongols? (*Although Yongle built the new capital of Bejing near where the Mongol capital of Dadu had been, he maintained his frontier guard within a newly fortified Great Wall that was now constructed much closer to the capital than had been the case in early times.*)

4. Why did China's maritime exploration end? (*Officials who were against the eunuchs and military expansion wanted to end maritime exploration. Also, the scholar Fan Ji wanted sea voyages to stop because he thought they were a waste of resources that could be used for agriculture and education. On balance, the Ming leaders believed that China could influence the world more positively by creating a good society at home than by pursuing military conquest abroad.*)

CRITICAL THINKING QUESTIONS

1. How did Ming Taizu show his interests in the common people? (*He improved schools in poor areas and set up schools in the villages, reintroduced quotas for recruiting officials so all regions would be represented, and reformed the country's laws to protect debtors, small merchants and women.*)

2. Why do you think the scholar-officials feared the eunuchs? (*Possible answer: They recognized the close contact the eunuchs had with the emperors, as well as the emperors' temptation to give the eunuchs more power and responsibility than they were supposed to. As well, the eunuchs operated outside of the normal structure of government. This led the scholar-officials to fear that the eunuchs might decide to take power for themselves.*)

3. How did Yongle's maritime expeditions benefit China? (*Through Yongle's six maritime expeditions, Chinese diplomats and merchants were able to visit Southeast Asia, as well as other states located in the South China Sea and the Indian Ocean, and the states of the Middle East and Africa. As a result, China was able to establish diplomatic relations with other countries and continue exchanges of goods and ideas even after the Silk Road began to decline.*)

THE ASIAN WORLD, 600–1500

THEN and NOW

Yongle stationed his frontier guard along a newly rebuilt Great Wall of China, which was much less distant from central China than the Qin-Han wall had been. Today the Great Wall no longer stands as a defense system for the military. The site is a popular tourist attraction and a symbol of strength and greatness for the Chinese nation.

LINKING DISCIPLINES

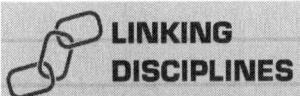

Science The Black Death that killed Zhu Yuanzhang's family was an epidemic that was spread by the fleas on rats. Have students work in pairs to research information on the Black Death epidemic. Then have pairs work together to compare the information they found.

LITERATURE CONNECTION

The Peony Pavilion is a Ming Dynasty masterpiece of Chinese opera by the great Chinese writer Tang Xianzu (1550–1616). Books on this masterpiece, such as Cyril Birch's translation (Indiana University Press, 2002), are available. There are also resources available online, such as www.dialnsa.edu/ecp/peony/ointro.htm, which gives an introduction to *The Peony Pavilion*, and offer other information about the history of Chinese opera.

LITERACY TIPS

In addition to using the suggestions in the Supporting Learning and Extending Learning sections, refer back frequently to pages 16–19 for strategies and advice from a literacy coach.

SOCIAL SCIENCES

Economics Maritime exploration in China during the 1400s affected China's economy in positive and negative ways. Trade helped the economy but the expeditions themselves were very expensive. Ask students to work in small groups to research the impact of maritime exploration on China's economy during the 1400s and discuss their findings with each other. One helpful website is www.china-inc.com/education/history/ming.html.

READING AND LANGUAGE ARTS

Reading Nonfiction Explain that biographical information is a form of nonfiction. Ask students to use the sequence of events chart (see reproducibles at the back of this guide) to organize the events in Zhu Yuanzhang's life. They should be sure to include events from all parts of his life.

Using Language History texts are typically written in the past tense. Have students work in pairs to review the chapter, making a list of the past-tense verbs they find as they read. Then ask the pairs to choose 15 of the words they found and make a two-column chart. In the second column, have students write the past-tense verbs they chose. In the first column, have students write the corresponding present-tense verb for each word in the second column.

WRITING

Description Ask students to imagine they are Zheng He and are on one of his maritime expeditions. Have them think about what they may see and discover in their travels and write a description of their experience. Students may need to do further research about Zheng He's travels as well as the places he visited.

SUPPORTING LEARNING

English Language Learners The chapter is full of words related to conflict, such as *rebelled*, *attacked*, *destroyed*, *struggle*, and *battle*. Have students work in pairs to make a list of words from the chapter that have a connotation of conflict. Then have each student choose five words from the list and write sentences using those words. Pairs of students can then regroup to share their sentences.

Struggling Readers Ask students to use the Venn diagram master to compare and contrast the two emperors discussed in the chapter, Ming Taizu and Yongle.

EXTENDING LEARNING

Enrichment Divide the class into two groups, one to represent the eunuchs and one to represent the scholar-officials. Then have each group research and prepare an argument for or against ending maritime trade based on which side the group they represent would take. Then have each group choose a few representatives to debate the issue before the class.

Extension Have students research the Chinese ships that were used in the maritime voyages of the early 1400s. Students can use the information they find to draw a diagram of one of these ships. One helpful website is www.time.com/time/asia/features/journey2001/greatship.html.

NAME _____ **DATE** _____

PRIMARY SOURCES

Directions

With a partner, read the passage below by Gao Qi, "The Tea Pickers." Then answer the questions that follow.

> The rain has passed over creeks and mountains, and the blue clouds are mild;
> In the thick shadows tea leaves are half-sprouted, and shoots are still short.
> The girls in silver hairpins sing back and forth;
> Looking at each other's baskets, they inquire: "Who has picked the most?"
> The fragrance of the tea leaves is still on their hands when they return;
> The highest grade tea will be first presented to the governor.
> Just cured in the bamboo brazier, the tea is so fresh—but they do not taste it;
> Packed into baskets, it will be sold to the **Hunan** merchants
> The mountain people do not know about growing rice and **millet**;
> Year after year they rely on the tea harvest season for their **sustenance**.

Notes on vocabulary:
Hunan, province of southeastern China
millet, a type of grain
sustenance, means of support

1. Describe this day that the poet discusses.
   _____

2. Do you think the tea pickers seem happy? Explain.
   _____
   _____

3. Write a line or a few words from the poem that gives an example of how each of the five senses is represented in the poem.
   taste _____
   smell _____
   hearing _____
   touch _____
   sight _____

CHAPTER BLM 12 — THE ASIAN WORLD, 600–1500

NAME _____ DATE _____

PRIMARY SOURCES

Directions

Read the quotations below. Then answer the questions that follow.

> I.
> Now all within the four seas are one family. . . . Let there be trade on the frontier to supply the country's needs and encourage distant people to come.
>
> —Yongle

> II.
> Although he [Zheng He] returned with wonderful, precious things, what benefit was it to the state?
>
> —Liu Daxia

1. In your own words, restate what Yongle is saying in the quotation above.

_____
_____
_____

2. Based on the quote from Yongle and the information from the chapter, answer Liu Daxia's question.

_____
_____
_____
_____
_____
_____
_____
_____

CHAPTER TEST 12

THE ASIAN WORLD, 600–1500

A. MULTIPLE CHOICE

Circle the letter of the best answer for each question.

1. All of the following are true of Ming Taizu **except**
   a. he was orphaned at the age of 16.
   b. he led his army to a victory at Suzhou and founded the Ming Dynasty.
   c. he improved the education system.
   d. he treated all of his officials and advisors fairly.

2. How did Yongle come to power?
   a. He took the throne from his nephew through a civil war.
   b. He inherited the throne from Ming Taizu.
   c. He was appointed by the scholar-officials.
   d. He was voted to the position by the eunuchs.

3. How did the scholar-officials feel about the eunuchs?
   a. They thought the eunuchs were extremely capable of leading the country.
   b. They feared the eunuchs were being given too much power by the emperor.
   c. They were envious of the eunuch's ability to travel on sea voyages.
   d. They were happy that the eunuchs were put in charge of the secret police force.

4. Which of the following goods did China **not** trade through its maritime trade?
   a. silk and cotton cloth
   b. tea
   c. woolen cloth
   d. porcelain

5. How did Zeng He come to know Zhu Di?
   a. He was taken prisoner and given to Zhu Di after a battle in Yunnan.
   b. They met while traveling on a maritime expedition.
   c. He was hired by Taizu to be Yongle's military commander.
   d. Zhu Di competed against him for the throne.

B. SHORT ANSWER

Answer these questions in two or three sentences.

6. What was significant about Admiral Zheng He's seventh voyage?

_____
_____
_____

C. ESSAY

Read the quotation from Ibn Battuta. Then answer the question.

> Among the inhabitants of China there are those who own numerous ships, on which they send their agents to foreign places. For nowhere in the world are to be found people richer than the Chinese.

On a separate piece of paper, write an essay explaining what led Ibn Battuta to this conclusion. Include information explaining the relationship between China's maritime trade and the country's wealth.

WRAP-UP TEST
The Asian World, 600–1500

NAME   **DATE**

Directions
Answer each of the following questions. Use additional paper if necessary

1. In an essay on a separate piece of paper, describe the three ways of thought that were combined and became known as Confucianism. Who came up with this new way of thinking and how did it change the make-up of the government?

2. Write an essay that explains how wood-block printing developed in China. Include one another Chinese invention in your explanation.

3. Write an essay comparing the Silk Road to the ocean trading routes. What were the risks and benefits of each? What did they have in common? When was one route better to use than another?

4. On a separate sheet of paper, describe agricultural developments during the Song period. What was their impact on Chinese farmers?

5. On a separate piece of paper, write an essay that explains how Buddhist and Confucian ideas influenced Mongol nomads to change their harsh plans for the Jin.

WRAP-UP TEST
THE ASIAN WORLD, 600–1500

NAME   **DATE**

6. On a separate piece of paper, describe the economy of southern China under Khubilai Khan and how it got to be that way.

7. Japan in the 12th century was a time of transition. Write a paragraph to explain how political power shifted from the emperor to a military general, or shogun. How did the shogun consolidate his power? What was the significance of his control over the military?

8. Write an essay describing the advances in learning and science that took place during King Segong's reign in Korea from 1419 to 1450.

9. On a separate piece of paper, write an essay that describes Ming Taizu's expectations of the scholar-official class and how he changed its membership.

10. Compare and contrast the different denominations of Buddhism (Pure Land, Nichiren, and Zen) that evolved in Japan.

SCORING RUBRIC

The reproducibles on the following pages have been adapted from this rubric for use as handouts and a student self-scoring activity, with added focus on planning, cooperation, revision and presentation. You may wish to tailor the self-scoring activity—for example, asking students to comment on how low scores could be improved, or focusing only on specific rubric points. Use the Library/Media Center Research Log to help students focus and evaluate their research for projects and assignments.

As with any rubric, you should introduce and explain the rubric before students begin their assignments. The more thoroughly your students understand how they will be evaluated, the better prepared they will be to produce projects that fulfill your expectations.

	ORGANIZATION	CONTENT	ORAL/WRITTEN CONVENTIONS	GROUP PARTICIPATION
4	• Clearly addresses all parts of the writing task. • Demonstrates a clear understanding of purpose and audience. • Maintains a consistent point of view, focus, and organizational structure, including the effective use of transitions. • Includes a clearly presented central idea with relevant facts, details, and/or explanations.	• Demonstrates that the topic was well researched. • Uses only information that was essential and relevant to the topic. • Presents the topic thoroughly and accurately. • Reaches reasonable conclusions clearly based on evidence.	• Contains few, if any, errors in grammar, punctuation, capitalization, or spelling. • Uses a variety of sentence types. • Speaks clearly, using effective volume and intonation.	• Demonstrated high levels of participation and effective decision making. • Planned well and used time efficiently. • Demonstrated ability to negotiate opinions fairly and reach compromise when needed. • Utilized effective visual aids.
3	• Addresses all parts of the writing task. • Demonstrates a general understanding of purpose and audience. • Maintains a mostly consistent point of view, focus, and organizational structure, including the effective use of some transitions. • Presents a central idea with mostly relevant facts, details, and/or explanations.	• Demonstrates that the topic was sufficiently researched. • Uses mainly information that was essential and relevant to the topic. • Presents the topic accurately but leaves some aspects unexplored. • Reaches reasonable conclusions loosely related to evidence.	• Contains some errors in grammar, punctuation, capitalization, or spelling. • Uses a variety of sentence types. • Speaks somewhat clearly, using effective volume and intonation.	• Demonstrated good participation and decision making with few distractions. • Planning and used its time acceptably. • Demonstrated ability to negotiate opinions and compromise with little aggression or unfairness.
2	• Addresses only parts of the writing task. • Demonstrates little understanding of purpose and audience. • Maintains an inconsistent point of view, focus, and/or organizational structure, which may include ineffective or awkward transitions that do not unify important ideas. • Suggests a central idea with limited facts, details, and/or explanations.	• Demonstrates that the topic was minimally researched. • Uses a mix of relevant and irrelevant information. • Presents the topic with some factual errors and leaves some aspects unexplored. • Reaches conclusions that do not stem from evidence presented in the project.	• Contains several errors in grammar, punctuation, capitalization, or spelling. These errors may interfere with the reader's understanding of the writing. • Uses little variety in sentence types. • Speaks unclearly or too quickly. May interfere with the audience's understanding of the project.	• Demonstrated uneven participation or was often off-topic. Task distribution was lopsided. • Did not show a clear plan for the project, and did not use time well. • Allowed one or two opinions to dominate the activity, or had trouble reaching a fair consensus.
1	• Addresses only one part of the writing task. • Demonstrates no understanding of purpose and audience. • Lacks a point of view, focus, organizational structure, and transitions that unify important ideas. • Lacks a central idea but may contain marginally related facts, details, and/or explanations.	• Demonstrates that the topic was poorly researched. • Does not discriminate relevant from irrelevant information. • Presents the topic incompletely, with many factual errors. • Did not reach conclusions.	• Contains serious errors in grammar, punctuation, capitalization, or spelling. These errors interfere with the reader's understanding of the writing. • Uses no sentence variety. • Speaks unclearly. The audience must struggle to understand the project.	• Demonstrated poor participation by the majority of the group. Tasks were completed by a small minority. • Failed to show planning or effective use of time. • Was dominated by a single voice, or allowed hostility to derail the project.

NAME _____   **PROJECT** _____

DATE _____

ORGANIZATION & FOCUS	CONTENT	ORAL/WRITTEN CONVENTIONS	GROUP PARTICIPATION

COMMENTS AND SUGGESTIONS

UNDERSTANDING YOUR SCORE

Organization: Your project should be clear, focused on a main idea, and organized. You should use details and facts to support your main idea.

Content: You should use strong research skills. Your project should be thorough and accurate.

Oral/Written Conventions: For writing projects, you should use good composition, grammar, punctuation, and spelling, with a good variety of sentence types. For oral projects, you should engage the class using good public speaking skills.

Group Participation: Your group should cooperate fairly and use its time well to plan, assign and revise the tasks involved in the project.

NAME _____ GROUP MEMBERS _____
_____
_____
_____

Use this worksheet to describe your project by finishing the sentences below.
For individual projects and writing assignments, use the "How I did" section.
For group projects, use both "How I did" and "How we did" sections.

The purpose of this project is to :

Scoring Key =   **4** – extremely well
3 – well
2 – could have been better
1 – not well at all

HOW I DID

I understood the purpose and requirements for this project...

I planned and organized my time and work...

This project showed clear organization that emphasized the central idea...

I supported my point with details and description...

I polished and revised this project...

I utilized correct grammar and good writing/speaking style...

Overall, this project met its purpose...

HOW WE DID

We divided up tasks...

We cooperated and listened to each other...

We talked through what we didn't understand...

We used all our time to make this project the best it could be...

Overall, as a group we worked together...

I contributed and cooperated with the team...

LIBRARY / MEDIA CENTER RESEARCH LOG

NAME _____

DUE DATE _____

What I Need to Find

I need to use:
- ☐ primary
- ☐ secondary

sources.

Places I Know to Look

Brainstorm: Other Sources and Places to Look

WHAT I FOUND

Title/Author/Location (call # or URL)

	Book/Periodical	Website	Other		Primary Source	Secondary Source		Suggestion	Library Catalog	Browsing	Internet Search	Web link		Rate each source from 1 (low) to 4 (high) in the categories below
							How I Found it							helpful / relevant
	☐	☐	☐		☐	☐		☐	☐	☐	☐	☐		____ ____
	☐	☐	☐		☐	☐		☐	☐	☐	☐	☐		____ ____
	☐	☐	☐		☐	☐		☐	☐	☐	☐	☐		____ ____
	☐	☐	☐		☐	☐		☐	☐	☐	☐	☐		____ ____
	☐	☐	☐		☐	☐		☐	☐	☐	☐	☐		____ ____
	☐	☐	☐		☐	☐		☐	☐	☐	☐	☐		____ ____

GRAPHIC ORGANIZERS

GUIDELINES

Reproducibles of seven different graphic organizers are provided on the following pages. These give your students a variety of ways to sort and order all the information they are receiving in this course. Use the organizers for homework assignments, classroom activities, tests, small group projects, and as ways to help the students take notes as they read.

1. Determine which graphic organizers work best for the content you are teaching. Some are useful for identifying main ideas and details; others work better for making comparisons, and so on.

2. Graphic organizers help students focus on the central points of the lesson while leaving out irrelevant details.

3. Use graphic organizers to give a visual picture of the key ideas you are teaching.

4. Graphic organizers can help students recall important information. Suggest students use them to study for tests.

5. Graphic organizers provide a visual way to show the connections between different content areas.

6. Graphic organizers can enliven traditional lesson plans and encourage greater interactivity within the classroom.

7. Apply graphic organizers to give students a concise, visual way to break down complex ideas.

8. Encourage students to use graphic organizers to identify patterns and clarify their ideas.

9. Graphic organizers stimulate creative thinking in the classroom, in small groups, and for the individual student.

10. Help students determine which graphic organizers work best for their purposes, and encourage them to use graphic organizers collaboratively whenever they can.

11. Help students customize graphic organizers as particular exercises dictate: e.g., more or fewer boxes, lines, or blanks than appear.

OUTLINE

MAIN IDEA: _____
_____
_____

    DETAIL: _____
    _____

    DETAIL: _____
    _____

    DETAIL: _____
    _____

MAIN IDEA: _____
_____
_____

    DETAIL: _____
    _____

    DETAIL: _____
    _____

    DETAIL: _____
    _____

Name _____ Date _____

MAIN IDEA MAP

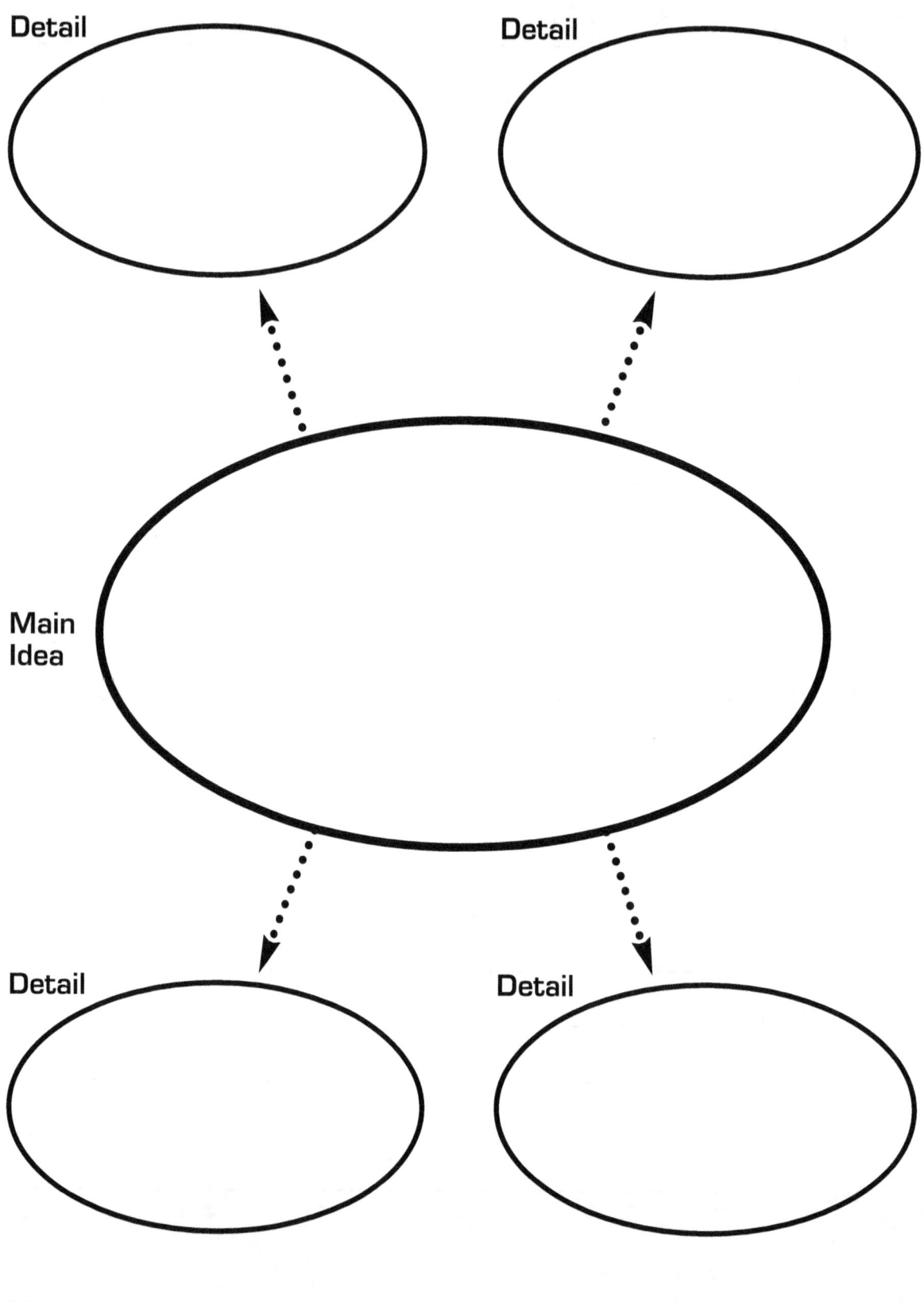

Name _____ Date _____

K-W-L CHART

K	W	L
What I Know	What I Want to Know	What I Learned

Name _____ Date _____

VENN DIAGRAM

Write differences in the circles. Write similarities where the circles overlap.

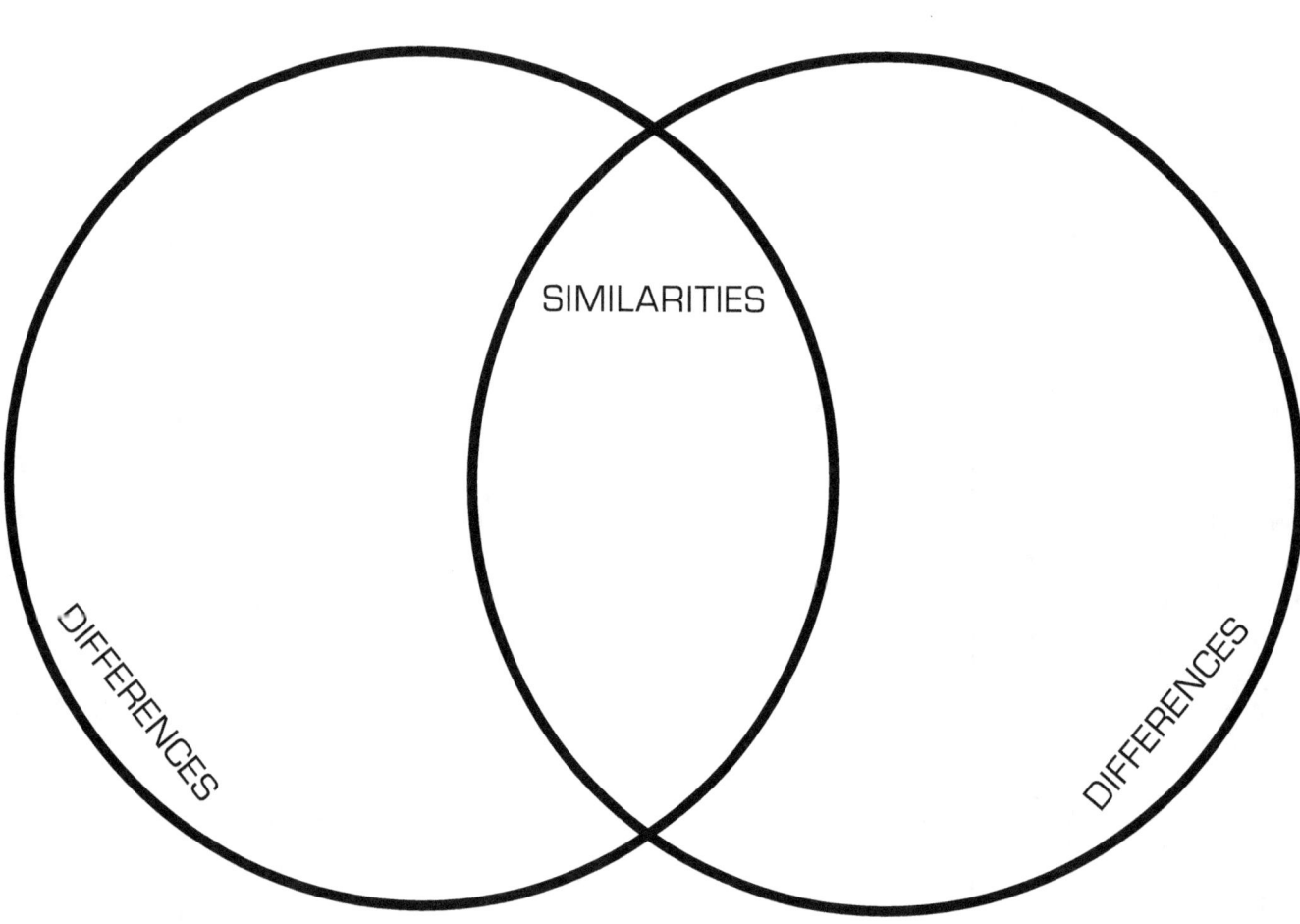

Name _____ Date _____

TIMELINE

DATE

EVENT Draw lines to connect the event to the correct year on the timeline.

Name _____ Date

SEQUENCE OF EVENTS CHART

Event

Next Event

Next Event

Next Event

Next Event

Name _____ Date _____

T-CHART

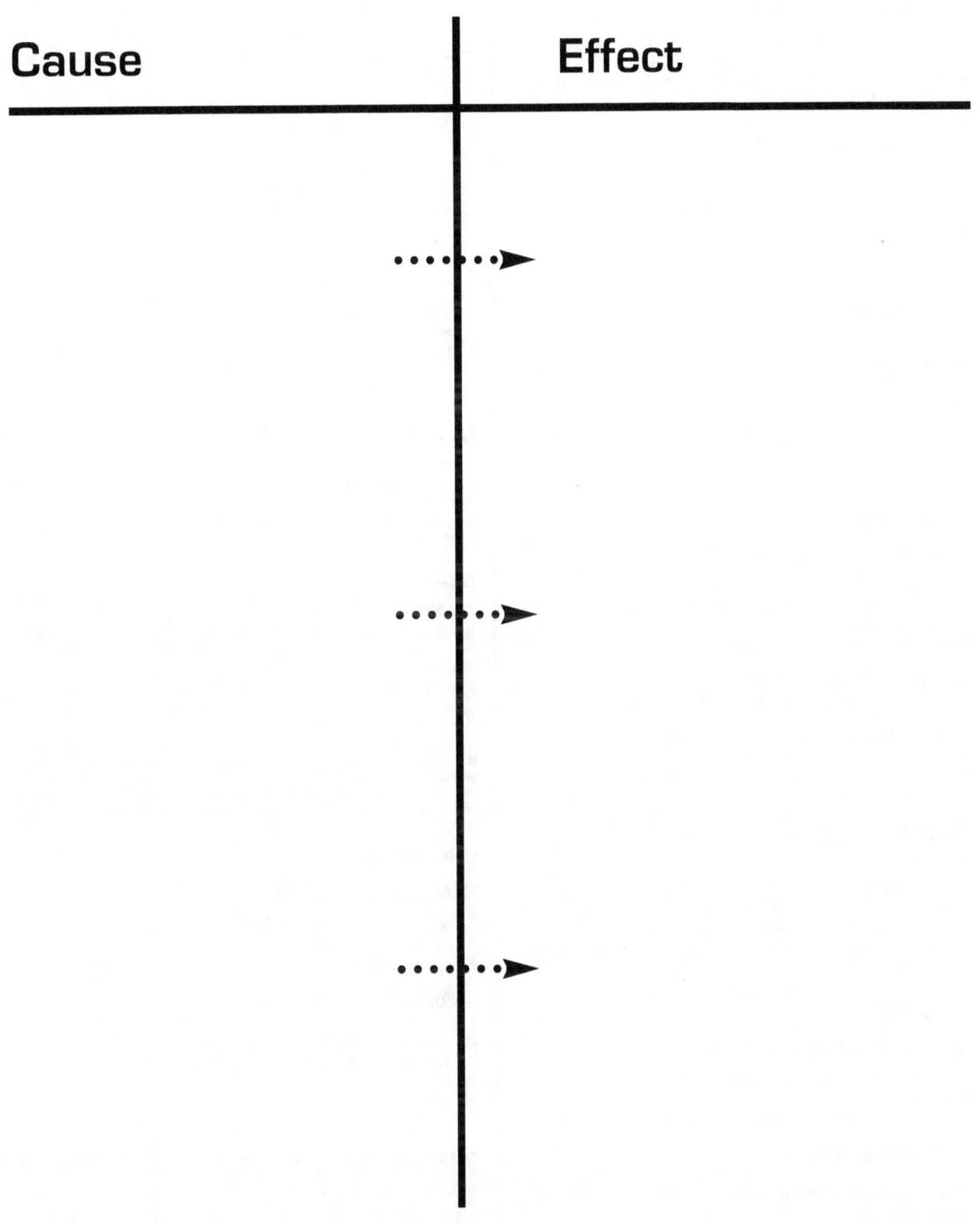

Name _____ Date _____

ANSWER KEY

CHAPTER 1

BLACKLINE MASTER 1

1. **and 2.** Check students' work against map on Student Edition page 25
3. Show routes along the eastern coast of India toward Southeast Asia
4. Show routes going by land along the Indus River, and then northwest towards the Persian Gulf and Red Sea, and through the Khyber Pass towards Central Asia
5. cotton cloth and spices

BLACKLINE MASTER 2

1. the belief that a virtuous ruler should rule people
2. Hanfeizi believes that a ruler must adjust his government to the age in which he rules; King Ashoka believes in benevolent rule no matter how difficult it is.
3. Governing an unruly people is like trying to steer a wild horse without using reins.
4. Answers will vary.

CHAPTER TEST

A. **1.** c; **2.** b; **3.** c; **4.** d.; **5.** c

B. **6.** He united China, standardized the money system, and built a wall to protect farmers from attacks from nomads.

7. Buddhism, which began in India, spread to Central Asia through the Silk Road and also east into China, and to Korea and Japan. Indian merchants, trading spices and cotton cloth, spread Hinduism northwest to Central Asia and east to regions in Southeast Asia.

C. Answers will vary.

CHAPTER 2

BLACKLINE MASTER 1

1. Yang Guifei being trampled to death by horses
2. Students may point out such details as the falling of hair combs, crown, bird-ornaments, and jade hairpins.
3. Answers will vary.

BLACKLINE MASTER 2

1. The tone of the first quotation is fearful and suspicious; the tone of the second is respectful and joyous.
2. It values Chinese culture above all others and reveres ancestors.
3. The Chinese viewed some foreigners as barbarians.
4. The writer is a monk, so his views might not be typical of a Japanese person who was not so religious.

CHAPTER TEST

A. **1.** b; **2.** c; **3.** b; **4.** b; **5.** a; **6.** d

B. **7.** They introduced Buddhism, drafted people in the army, and built the Grand Canal.

8. They had to face corruption, foreign invasions, and tax evasion.

C. Essays should point out that China was too big and diverse to hold together forever; in addition, dynasties begin to become corrupt after a while.

CHAPTER 3

BLACKLINE MASTER 1

1.–3. Compare students' work against map on Student Edition page 46
4. Harsha's empire ended at his death, 647
5. start at the capital at Nalanda, and draw arrows going from east to west

BLACKLINE MASTER 2

1. Answers will vary.
2. Kumar, the god of war, has beaten a demon named Taraka.
3. Answers will vary.

CHAPTER TEST

A. **1.** b; **2.** a; **3.** c; **4.** b; **5.** d

B. **6.** The Arabs learned certain mathematic concepts from the Indians.

7. Christianity and Judaism believe in one god, as does Islam, but Hinduism and Buddhism believe in many gods.

C. Answers will vary, but students should mention the conversion of Hindus and others to Islam, the rule by Muslim leaders in some parts of India, and the lack of permanent impact of Islam in many regions of India.

CHAPTER 4

BLACKLINE MASTER 1

1. Alexandria and Baghdad
2. because of the Himalayas, which were impossible for caravans to pass through
3. by caravan, unlike the ocean routes, which carried goods by ship
4. No; they could take their wares part of the way, sell them to another merchant, and then return home. The silk could change many hands before reaching its final destination.
5. **a)** China; west to central Asia and the Mediterranean
   b) Middle East, using raw silk from China
   c) China; west to Central Asia and the Middle East

BLACKLINE MASTER 2

1. Answers will vary.
2. They were not permanent rulers who inherited their positions, but were selected by merit.
3. Kings were probably removed because they were thought to be responsible for natural disasters.

CHAPTER TEST

A. **1.** c; **2.** d; **3.** a; **4.** c; **5.** b

B. **6.** In the late summer, the monsoon winds blew from west to east, allowing ships to sail from Arabia to India. The ships would make their return trip when the monsoon winds changed direction.

7. He was the king of the Javanese kingdom of Mataram. He made water control and irrigation systems to increase rice production, and also made improvements to the kingdom's main seaport.

C. Trade increases the flow of ideas among peoples, enriching them by exposing them to new beliefs and technologies. For example, Muslims used Chinese papermaking techniques to print the Quran on paper, extending their beliefs to many more people. Non-Buddhists were exposed to Buddhist beliefs from Buddhist temples, sculptures, and wall paintings that they saw along the Silk Road.

CHAPTER 5

BLACKLINE MASTER 1

1. a ceremony in which Genji symbolically becomes a man
2. They are sorry to see Genji's beautiful hair cut.
3. She has probably died.

BLACKLINE MASTER 2

1. Quotation from Ki no Tsurayuki
2. Quotation from Sei Shonagon
3. *Possible answer*: learning, fairness, loyalty, obedience, sincerity, courage, cooperation, friendliness
4. Answers will vary.
5. Answers will vary.

CHAPTER TEST

A. **1.** d; **2.** c; **3.** d; **4.** b; **5.** c

B. **6.** Officials were corrupt; common people suffered from high rents and taxes, and many farmers were sold into slavery to pay their debts.

7. They dominated the throne indirectly, accumulated large estates on which they did not pay taxes, and allowed other families to build up military strength in the countryside.

C. Answers will vary.

ANSWER KEY

CHAPTER 6
BLACKLINE MASTER 1
1.–2. Check students' work against the map on Student Edition page 79
3. Kaifeng
4. Payment was in the form of silver and silk, sent north to Liao
5. The Song also sent well-born women north as wives for the Liao emperor and his officials.
6. The Song sent the Xixia dynasty yearly gifts of silk, silver, and tea.

BLACKLINE MASTER 2
1. *Possible answer:* The painter must know the subject so well that he has a fully formed image of it in his mind's eye before he begins to paint it.
2. All three shed their skins.
3. A skilled painter is compared to a falcon attacking a rabbit.
4. *Possible answer:* Sometimes your mind knows how to do something, but you still can't do it because you haven't practiced enough.

CHAPTER TEST
A. 1. c; 2. c; 3. b; 4. d; 5. b; 6. b
B. 7. Rulers of the Jin dynasty to the north moved south into Song territory, cutting Chinese merchants off from the Silk Road. In response, they expanded into the overseas trade with Southeast Asia.
8. Farmers began using seeds for rice that opened earlier, so it could be harvested sooner, allowing Chinese farmers to grow much more food than they could before.
C. Answers will vary.

CHAPTER 7
BLACKLINE MASTER 1
1.–3. Check students' work against the map on Student Edition page 91
4. Mount Burkhan
5. Zhongdu (on the site of present-day Beijing)

BLACKLINE MASTER 2
1. *Possible answer:* to explain to people what was legal and what was illegal
2. The Muslim didn't know about the law and so the Great Khan felt sorry for him.
3. Answers will vary.

CHAPTER TEST
A. 1. c; 2. a; 3. d; 4. b; 5. d; 6. c
B. 7. No; he could not create permanent government institutions which were needed to run an empire and hold onto power
8. He allied with the Khitans and besieged the Jin capital of Zhongdu for two years; the city surrendered in 1215. It was the first Mongol conquest in China within the Great Wall.
C. *Possible answers:*
1. The Mongol tribe became small and poor.
2. He was poisoned and died.
3. His family's wealth increased.
4. He was pronounced Genghis Khan.
5. Scribes wrote down Genghis Khan's decrees as laws.
6. The Mongols conquered the Khwarazmi and slaughtered most of them.
7. The people of North China were protected somewhat from harsh Mongol rule.

CHAPTER 8
BLACKLINE MASTER 1
1. God
2. the Divine, or God
3. yourself
4. your body
5. That God is within you

BLACKLINE MASTER 2
1. They are hoping that the sultan will enrich their lives and give them wealth.
2. The sultan could kill anyone at any time.
3. The sultan loves to shed blood. He is known for his cruelty, severity.
4. The sultan is generous and brave. He is a humble man and devoted to truth and his religion.

CHAPTER TEST
A. 1. a; 2. c; 3. b; 4. d; 5. a
B. 6. Aybak built Middle-Eastern style mosques and made Persian the official language of his government. People who had dealings with the Muslim government or who had converted to Islam, began wearing Muslim-style clothing, the women dressed more modestly, and the Muslims ate beef (which shocked the Hindus, for whom cows were considered sacred animals).
7. Raziha took over the sultanate when Aybak's heir, Iltumish, died in 1236. She dressed and behaved like a man, and people accepted her leadership at first. Then she was driven out when more traditional Muslims disapproved of her behavior. In attempting to recapture the throne, she was killed after the battle.
C. Many Hindus converted to Islam and adopted Muslim clothing and music styles. Intermarriage between Hindus and Muslims also became more common, and Muslims became more comfortable with Hindu religious practices.)

CHAPTER 9
BLACKLINE MASTER 1
1. Venice, Shangdu, Dadu
2. Shangdu and Dadu. He built two capitals so he could spend the hot summer months in the cooler mountains up north (Shangdu). The rest of the year the government was located in Dadu.
3. Beijing
4. extension of the Grand Canal to bring riches and other goods from the southern agricultural regions to the new capital at Dadu.
5. Mediterranean Sea, Persian Gulf, Indian Ocean, South China Sea, Black Sea

BLACKLINE MASTER 2
1. The system made the government run more smoothly and was very convenient. No other rulers had such a system.
2. Today everyone, and not just rulers or leaders, can send messages, or mail, to people through the postal system. Mail is transported by truck and airplane and not horses to get to its destination. Today people also use the computer to send e-mail, which delivers the message instantly.

CHAPTER TEST
A. 1. d; 2. a; 3. b; 4. c;
B. 5. He built an extension of the Grand Canal, designed and built two new capital cities in China, and divided the population of China into four groups based on ethnic and geographic background.
6. The Mongol leadership was resented because the Mongols kept themselves separate from Han Chinese society, taking the highest government jobs and discouraging intermarriage. Also, bad administration, famine, and popular unrest further weakened the dynasty.
C. 7. Answers will vary.

THE ASIAN WORLD, 600–1500

ANSWER KEY

CHAPTER 10
BLACKLINE MASTER 1
Possible answers:
1. If you do not claim to belong to any particular place, everywhere you go will seem like where you belong.
2. The poem represents the Zen idea of simplicity in life and absence of complications.

BLACKLINE MASTER 2
1. The moonlight looks brilliant when it is shining into the house of a good and peaceful man.
2. *Possible answer:* someone who prefers a simple life, likely a Zen Buddhist
3. *Possible answer:* someone who is not as in touch with his spiritual side and who is attached to his possessions
4. Answers will vary but should include that the house would be simple and without many ornaments.

CHAPTER TEST
A. 1. a; 2. d; 3. b; 4. c; 5. a

B. 6. *Answers will vary but may include:*
Nichiren angered the Hojo leaders by predicting the Mongol attack and gained followers, which threatened the Hojo rulers.
7. It appealed to military aristocrats because of its focus on self-discipline and getting rid of mental distractions.

C. *Answers will vary but may include:*
Japan was able to trade goods with China, which helped improve the economy of Japan. Japan learned more about Zen Buddhism and the people were able to learn new skills in zen arts.

CHAPTER 11
BLACKLINE MASTER 1
1.–3. Check students' work against the map on Student Edition page 139
4. Old capital was Kaesong; new capital became Hanyang.
5. Hanyang was a better location because it was centrally located and more convenient for the Korean people. It was also near a seaport, not landlocked as was Kaesong, which made the kingdom better able to participate in ocean trade.

BLACKLINE MASTER 2
Essays should include that the people in the passage were considered less than the elite and wanted to have equal status, while the people of the Choson dynasty had more equity, as evidenced in the quotation by the Confucian advisor regarding the distribution of land and the quote from General Yi regarding the people's wishes.

CHAPTER TEST
A. 1. d; 2. a; 3. c; 4. b

B. 5. Wang Kon founded the kingdom of Koryo, then a Mongol ambassador to Korea was killed. After General Yi Songgye seized the Korean capital, Sejong became king.
6. It allowed trade between Korea, China, and Mongolia, and Koreans were able to travel to China and learn new ideas and information.

C. Answers will vary but should include that Korea began trade of goods to and from China and Mongolia, government was influenced by Confucian principles, and Korea was able to use ideas from China to make new inventions (wood block printing inspired metal-type printing).

CHAPTER 12
BLACKLINE MASTER 1
1. It has just finished raining and the temperature is mild.
2. Yes, they sing to each other and they joke with each other about who picked the most tea.
3. *Possible answers:*
   Taste: . . . the tea is so fresh—but they do not taste it;
   Smell: the fragrance of the tea leaves is still on their hands.
   Hearing: The girls . . . sing back and forth.
   Touch: Packed into baskets . . .
   Sight: In the thick shadows tea leaves are half sprouted . . .

BLACKLINE MASTER 2
1. Answers will vary.
2. Answers will vary but may include that the state would benefit from the voyages because the voyages were a way for China to get what it needed, see other lands, and unify the people of the countries surrounding the seas upon which the Chinese ships traveled by establishing diplomatic relations with those countries. This was also an opportunity to explore new places and acquire new things.

CHAPTER TEST
A. 1. d; 2. a; 3. b; 4. c; 5. a

B. 6. Its purpose was to maintain peace and good governance in the Indian Ocean. It was also Zheng's largest voyage, and his last: he died during the voyage to East Africa.

C. Answers will vary.

WRAP-UP TEST
1. The three ways of thought are Legalism, Daoism, and Confucius's emphasis on education and virtue as the basis of good government. Legalism said that if laws were clear and specific, everyone would do exactly what he or she was supposed to do. Daoism said that everything in the universe follows a force (called "the Way") that lies behind all processes, and Daoists believed there could be a ruler so tuned in to the power of the Way that he could rule the world without even trying. Confucius taught that government service should not be based on noble birth, but on intelligence, education, and virtue. The Han ruler Emperor Wu combined these three ways of thought. In the Han dynasty Confucianism led to the selection of public officials by examinations that tested their knowledge and virtue.
2. At the time that Buddhism arrived in China, Buddhist scriptures had to be copied out by hand. Because the process was long and slow, it was expensive to buy copies of the scriptures. In the early Tang period an unknown Buddhist craftsperson thought to carve words and pictures (in mirror image) onto smooth blocks of wood. The wood blocks could then be coated with ink, and the images transferred to a sheet of paper (which the Chinese had also invented, during the Han dynasty). The invention of wood-block printing made it possible to reproduce multiple copies of anything quickly and cheaply.
3. *Answers should include these points:* The Silk Road was shorter in miles but much slower, because travel over land was slow. Caravans were in danger of being attacked by bandits and robbers, or of getting lost. They were not safe in times of war. Ocean trade was sometimes interrupted by pirates; it was also dependent on the monsoon seasons.
4. The Song government introduced seeds of Southeast Asian rice that got ripe early. Chinese farmers bred the seeds to grow in their particular soil and climate. Landowning scholar-officials wrote and published manuals to spread the news of these improved rice varieties. Because the new rice could be harvested sooner than the old rice, farmers were able to grow more crops each year.
5. The Mongols had planned to punish the Jin for resisting them and to turn north China into pastureland for themselves. A nobleman who had served the Jin dynasty used the Confucian principle of "humaneness" and the Buddhist idea of "right action" to convince the Mongol leaders not to attack. Instead, he persuaded them to rule China using Chinese methods and helped them to set up a system for taxing farmers rather than plundering them.
6. International trade across the South China Sea and the Indian Ocean thrived in southern China, and market towns and manufacturing centers prospered more than ever before. The Yuan administration forbade southerners from holding official positions, so many turned to trade as a way to make a living. Furthermore, the southerners paid relatively low taxes, so they could invest their money in commerce.
7. The first shogun, Yoritomo, kept the emperor on the throne but retained power by being head of the military. He consolidated power by allying with other clan leaders and giving them estates to manage.
8. He created an education system and set up the Hall of Worthies, where inventions were on display. He established a royal observatory for studying the night sky. He also emphasized decency and good morals among his officials and oversaw the creation of a new Korean writing system.
9. Ming Taizu expected scholars and officials to meet the needs of the common people. They had to be more than just book smart, they also had to understand worldly matters, such as economic conditions in the countryside. He changed the membership of the scholar-official class by making it possible for men from different social and economic backgrounds—not just the wealthy or well-born—to become part of it. He did this by establishing public schools in the provinces and counties and encouraging local scholars to set up schools in the villages. When many more rich students passed the civil-service exams than poor ones, he suspended the exams until he was sure that every student would have an equal chance to pass.

ANSWER KEY

10. *Similarities:* All emphasized enlightenment and an idea of liberation or salvation from the suffering of an illusory world, but differed in the requirements for that enlightenment.
Differences: Pure Land—felt the only requirement was to rely on the mercy of the Buddha of Infinite Light. Nichiren Buddhism—stressed the importance of the Lotus Sutra. Zen—stressed meditation and enlightenment from within.

ANSWERS FOR THE STUDENT STUDY GUIDE

CHAPTER 1
Check students' responses for accuracy.
Siddartha Gautama (about 550–461 BCE): the Buddha ("Enlightened One"), founder of Buddhism
Kong Zhongni (551–479 BCE) or Kongzi: Chinese philosopher and teacher known in the West as Confucius
Laozi, "Old Master": legendary 6th century BCE found of Daosim
Qin Shi Huangdi (258–210 BCE): unifier and first emperor of China
Mahavira: Founder of Jainism in the 6th–5th centuries BCE
Ashoka: Indian king of the Maurya dynasty who ruled about 272–232 BCE
Emperor Wu: most powerful of the Han rulers; ruled from 140–87 BCE

Word Bank
1. exploitation **2.** meditate **3.** nomadic **4.** rituals **5.** subcontinent **6.** frugally

Word Play radical; Check students' sentences.

Critical Thinking: Drawing Conclusions
1. *Possible answer:* He was very unusual. He questioned the life that people led and tried to figure out how their lives could be improved. He invented a whole new religion to explain what he experienced and discovered through meditation.
2. *Possible answer:* It would be orderly and respectful. Everyone would be fair, trusting, and obedient.
3. *Possible answer:* Using written merit exams upset the old way of doing things in which officials inherited their positions because they came from noble families. Now officials were chosen for what they could do, not for who they were

Critical Thinking: Compare and Contrast
Buddhism: c, h
Hindusim: b, e, I
Both: a, d, f, g

Working with Primary Sources
1. Answers may vary. Possible words: love, respect, joy, admiration, worship
2. Dharma is the path of truth and duty taught by the Buddha as the way people should live. Believers say followers of the dharma will escape the constant cycle of rebirth and human suffering and become part of the force of the universe.
3. The Lotus Sutra helped Buddhism become accepted in China.

CHAPTER 2
Cast of Characters
Sui Wendi, personal name Yang Jian (541–604): Chinese emperor and founder of Sui dynasty
Li Yuan (566–635): founder and first emperor of China's Tang dynasty
Tang Taizong, personal name Li Shimin: second emperor of China's Tang dynasty; ruled 626–648
Xuanzang (600–664): Chinese Buddhist pilgrim to India
Wu Zhao (625–706): imperial concubine who became China's only female emperor
Tang Xuanzong: Chinese emperor during Tang dynasty who ruled 713–756; had a tragic affair with concubine Yang Guifei
Wang Wei (699–761): Chinese Buddhist poet and painter
Li Bai (701–762): Chinese Tang dynasty poet
Du Fu (712–770): Chinese Tang dynasty poet

Word Bank
1. regent **2.** regime **3.** campaign **4.** famine **5.** imperial **6.** stroke

Word Play conspiracy; Check students' sentences.

Critical Thinking: Compare and Contrast
Answers will vary.

Critical Thinking: Drawing Conclusions
Possible answer: Wu Zhao had already been acting as emperor for some time. She had proved herself such a powerful ruler that people were either afraid to challenge her or so impressed with her skill they chose not to challenge her.

Working with Primary Sources
1. Answers will vary.
2. He was alive and unhurt and as he said, "Life is the most precious thing in existence."
3. Answers will vary.

Write About It
Answers will vary, but students should understand that the poet is commenting on the way wars continue through the generations.

Working with Primary Sources
1. sad in first two, content in the third
2. Guanxu
3. both by Du Fu
4. The An Lushan rebellion and fighting that separated him from his family

CHAPTER 3
Cast of Characters
Mahadeviyakka: Indian woman religious poet
Harsha Vardhana: north Indian conqueror, "king of kings"
Muhammad: prophet, founder of Islam
Muhammad ibn Qasim: Arab prince, conquered Indian province of Sind
Mahmud of Gazni: Muslim ruler of Afghanistan, invaded India
Bhoj: Indian philosopher-king who ruled 1018–1055
Muhammad Ghori: Persian ruler, conquered northern India
Qutb-ud-Ddn Aybak: first sultan of Delhi
Kalidasa: influential author of plays, stories, and poetry.

Word Bank
1. tolerant **2.** salvation **3.** access **4.** realm **5.** clarity **6.** decisive **7.** diverse

Word Play benefactors; Check students' sentences.

What Happened When?
590 - Harsha born
610 - Muhammad's teachings became Islam
632 - Muhammad died
647 - Harsha died
712 - Muhammad ibn Qasim conquered cities of Sind
1004 - Mahmud of Gazni seized Panjab
1030 - Mahmud of Gazni died
1173 - Muhammad Ghori became governor of Afghanistan
1192 - Muhammad Ghori won decisive battle in India
1202 - Muhammad Ghori became sultan of Ghur
1206 - Muhammad Ghori died and his general was appointed the first sultan of Delhi

Critical Thinking
1. The text says that she left home against her parents' will, so they were probably unhappy with her decision. They may have been worried about her safety or wanted her to lead a more conventional life.
2. Because Mecca was a trading center, lots of different kinds of people passed through it, including Jews and Christians, whose idea of one god was adopted by Muhammad.
3. *Possible answer:* He had sympathy for Jewish, Christians, and Zoroastrian religions, which believed in one god. He may have been a fair-minded person who thought everyone deserved to worship as they wished and so left Buddhists and Hindus alone, or he may have had more practical reasons and wanted to keep the peace.

Working with Primary Sources
1. God is immortal, but mortals such as husband die, so the speaker wanted to devote herself to God.
2. Their value or prize is hidden.
3. a belief in God, which lies hidden in the heart
4. Answers will vary.

Write About It
Answers will vary, but rulers should include Muhammad ibn Qasim, Mahmud of Gazni, Muhammad Ghori, and Hutb-ud-Din Aybak. Students should note the adoption of Islam by some Indians.

ANSWER KEY

Working with Primary Sources
1. The writer enjoyed the festival and described it as taking place in a pleasant setting.
2. A tree
3. The speaker believes that because subjects depend on their king, they can only thrive when the king is strong.
4. Possible answer: the learning, talent, and cooperation he witnessed impressed him.

CHAPTER 4
Cast of Characters
Ibn Sina: Islamic scientist and scholar, known in medieval Europe as Avicenna
Airlangga: Ruler of Mataram Empire in Indonesia

Word Bank
1. caravan 2. maritime 3. verdant 4. aromatic 5. supple

Word Play dominated; Check students' sentences.

Critical Thinking: Main Ideas
1. Paragraph 4: Down-the-line trade allowed goods to travel farther than people, but the price increased.
2. Paragraph 7: "Perhaps most importantly of all, the Silk Road provided a means for the spread of religious ideas."
3. Paragraph 13: "Trade in the Indian Ocean depended on the monsoons . . ."

Critical Thinking: Supporting Details
1. goods traveled farther than merchants; silk would become more expensive each time it changed hands;
2. many merchants were Buddhists; large Buddhist temples were built on the Silk Road; other religions traveled along the Silk Road
3. monsoon direction determined when ships sailed where; summer monsoons blow from west to east; ships would return home when seasons changed and the winds blew in the other direction.

Working with Primary Sources
1. the royal library of Bukhara
2. *Possible answers:* excited, impressed, awed.
3. The library, which was in Bukhara, had books by Greek authors, so trade with Greece or with a country that traded with Greece got them there.

Write About It
Answers will vary.

Working with Primary Sources
1. trade; faraway places
2. They both counsel good treatment of merchants.
3. Since ideas flowed with goods, the ruler's good reputation would soon be known far and wide.
4. *Possible answer:* tropical

CHAPTER 5
Cast of Characters
Kim Wonjong: king of Silla Kingdom, Korea
Sondok: queen of Silla Kingdom, Korea, daughter of Kim Wonjong,
Suiko: queen of Japan installed in 587
Shotoku: Japanese prince, regent for Queen Suiko; proclaimed 17-Article Constitution
Fujiwara Michinaga: head of powerful Japanese aristocratic clan
Murasaki Shikibu: Japanese woman writer, author of *The Tale of Genji*.

Word Bank
1. aristocracy 2. status 3. succession 4. oppressing 5. lacquer 6. hybrid

Word Play doctrines; Check students' sentences.

What Happened When?
514 Kim Wonjong becomes king of Silla
535 Kim Wonjong makes Buddhism official religion of Korea
552 Buddhism comes to Japan
587 Suiko becomes queen of Japan
604 Prince Sotoku's constitution changes government of Japan
632 Queen Sondok becomes ruler of Silla
646 Taika reforms in Japan
795 Japan capital established at Kyoto
1010 Lady Murasaki writes *The Tale of Genji*
1185 Heian period comes to an end in Japan

Working with Primary Sources
1. sleeping on a hillside
2. *Possible answer:* that life goes on even when we are unaware of it.
3. *Possible answers:* calm, peaceful, resigned.
4. *Possible answer:* She values surface appearances rather than more important things.

Write About It
Answers will vary.

Working with Primary Sources
1. Japanese regent who ruled Japan through his family until 1027
2. He's proud because of his power over ruling Japan.
3. Because of his family connections, he effectively ruled Japan for 30 years.

CHAPTER 6
Cast of Characters
Yelü Abaoji: Khitan ruler, founder and first emperor of Liao dynasty
Zhao Kuangyin founder of Song dynasty, also known as Song Taizu (suhng-tie-dzoo)
Zhu Xi Song dynasty scholar and philosopher
Fan Kuan Song dynasty landscape painter who became a Daoist hermit
Li Qingzhao Song dynasty woman poet

Word Bank
1. masts 2. emulate 3. modify 4. rudders 5. suspended 6. encroach 7. catapults

Word Play hermit; Check students' sentences.

What Happened When?
907 Abaoji extended his authority after the collapse of the Tang dynasty.
960 Zhao Kuangyin established the Song dynasty.
1038 Tangut people set up Xixia dynasty.
1044 The Song agreed to send annual tribute to Xixia rulers.
1126 The Song government left northern China and moved to a new capital in the south.

Critical Thinking
1. *Possible answer:* They would no longer be able to defend themselves effectively and would be too weak to conquer new territory.
2. *Possible answer:* They didn't think their students would understand the ideas in the books when they were younger.
3. *Possible answer:* very tough; the Jin beat them so badly the Song had to move south and establish a new capital.
4. *Possible answer:* She was highborn and married to an important man, and she must also have had a particularly strong and independent nature.

Working with Primary Sources
1. *Possible answer:* The first poem is nostalgic, sad, and wistful; the second is cheerful and proud.
2. *Possible answer:* The first poem shows how important nature was to the Song and how cultured the Song were; the second also shows the importance of nature, but also shows the importance of tiny feet to a woman's beauty.
3. *Possible answer:* Jade was precious to the Chinese, so the comparison was very positive.

Write About It
Possible answer: Exams were held every three years at local, provincial, and national levels, but only a few candidates were able to pass at each level. Places were reserved for candidates from each area of the country. Even though examinations were open to everyone, successful candidates came from relatively wealthy families that hired tutors to make sure that their children would be well educated and stand a good chance of passing. Learning was highly valued and governing was thought to be the responsibility of well-educated people.

Working with Primary Sources
1. No matter what work you do, do it as well as you can.
2. ones that capture the beauty of particular places
3. so that the viewer would look at it carefully and judge it according to an ideal of beauty
4. He admired the waiter: how quickly the waiter served, how many dishes he carried, and how he remembered which dishes everyone ordered.

ANSWER KEY

CHAPTER 7

Cast of Characters
Genghis Khan: Mongol world conqueror; original name Temujin
Ho'elun: mother of Genghis Khan
Borte: wife of Genghis Khan
Qiu Chuji: Chinese Daoist priest who visited Genghis Khan
Jochi: eldest son of Genghis Khan
Ogodei: son of Genghis Khan, Great Khan 1229–1241
Mongke: grandson of Genghis Khan, Great Khan 1251–1259
Khubilai Khan: grandson of Genghis Khan, founded Yuan dynasty of China
Rashid al-Din: Muslim statesman and historian

Word Bank
1. plunder **2.** domination **3.** suppress **4.** humility **5.** confederation

Word Play
clan; Check students' sentences.

Critical Thinking
fact: 1, 3, 5, 6
opinion: 2, 4, 7, 8, 9, 10

Working with Primary Sources
1. Answers will vary.
2. *Possible answers:* Genghis Khan felt at one with his people, even though he probably lived more comfortably than most of them. Genghis Khan wanted to appear humble.
3. *Possible answers:* He was relentless in his wish to conquer his enemies right up to his final days.
4. Answers will vary.

Write About It
Answers will vary.

Working with Primary Sources
1. The tone of the first excerpt is neutral and the second complimentary.
2. The tone is horrified.
3. The first two quotes were written by someone who actually spent time with Genghis Khan. The English historian may not have actually seen any part of the Mongol Empire or any Mongolian people. If he did, his prejudice against them prevented him from observing what he saw objectively.
4. Whether the writer had actually visited the Mongol Empire and how much time he spent there; reasons the writer might be biased against or for the Mongols.

CHAPTER 8

Cast of Characters
1. f **2.** i **3.** a **4.** g **5.** c **6.** b **7.** j **8.** d **9.** e **10.** h

Word Bank
1. ambitious **2.** accommodate **3.** conscientious **4.** salvaged **5.** deference **6.** successive

Word Play
contemporary; Check students' sentences.

What Happened When?
1210 Aybak was killed by his polo pony.
1236 Iltumish died and left the throne to his son. Then Raziya took the throne for herself.
1240 Raziya launched an attack on Delhi to recover the throne. She was killed in battle.
1296 Ala-ud-din became sultan.
1316 Tughluq, an ex-slave, became sultan.
1333 Ibn Battuta arrived in Delhi.
1336 Vijayanagara was founded.
1398 Timur Leng attacked Delhi.
c. 1440 The poet Kabir was born.
1565 Vijayanagara was destroyed.

Critical Thinking
Fact 3, 5
Opinion 1, 2, 4

All Over the Map
1.–2. Check students' work against map on Student Edition page 106.
3. Muslim icon goes with Sultanate region
4. Hindu icon goes with Vijayanagara Kingdom
5. Jamuna River

Write About It
Delhi was attacked and plundered by Timur Leng; Vijayanagara prospered from trade with Southeast Asia and remained stable because it established a strong mercenary army.

Comprehension
1. Hindus were forced to find ways to accommodate the changes.
2. The side of Raziya and her husband lost and the two were killed trying to flee the battle scene.
3. Ibn Battuta was relieved and believed this saved his life.
4. The city enjoyed peace and security for a century and a half.
5. Many Muslim and Hindu people of his time thought of Kabir as a saint.

CHAPTER 9

Cast of Characters
Marco Polo: Italian explorer who traveled to China.
Khubilai Khan: founder of the Yuan dynasty who reorganized China and under whose rule the Mongols retained power
Liu Bingzhong: religious scholar who suggested the name Yuan as the name of Khubilai Khan's dynasty
Guo Shoujing: well-known mathematician, astronomer, and engineer who designed the Grand Canal of China
Chabi: the wife of Khubilai Khan
Chengzong: Yuan emperor after Khubilai Khan who made peace with the Turks
Renzong: the forth Yuan emperor who reinstituted the examination system
Zhao Mengfu: head of the Hanlin academy under Renzong

Word Bank
1. dynasty **2.** cavalry

Word Play
tributary; Check students' sentences.

Critical Thinking
1. after **2.** after **3.** after **4.** before **5.** before **6.** after **7.** before **8.** after

Working with Primary Sources
1. Answers will vary
2. Yes, because he shows he respects all the religions, an attitude that would help him rule peacefully.

CHAPTER 10

Cast of Characters
Taira Kiyomori: powerful Taira leader of Japan whose army crushed the Minamota
Yoritomo: Minamoto leader, brother of Yoshitsune, and first shogun ruler who founded a military government that lasted almost seven centuries
Yoshitune: Minamoto leader and brother of Yoritomo who after losing a quarrel with his brother committed ritual suicide
Shinran: the Pure Land Master, a monk who was exiled for his ideas that evildoers were more acceptable than good people to Amitabha and that monks should marry
Nichiren: Buddhist teacher who created the Lotus sutra form of Buddhism and was later exiled for insulting the Hojo regents
Godaigo: emperor who tried to recover political authority for the imperial throne
Ashikaga Takauji: military commander sent to dethrone Godaigo but chose to join his forces instead and later claimed himself shogun
Muso Soseki: Zen master who encouraged friendly relations with China

Word Bank
1. disciples **2.** exiled **3.** abdicate

Word Play
meditation; Check students' sentences.

Critical Thinking
1. a, b; **2.** a, c; **3.** a, d; **4.** b, d

What Happened When?
1181 Taira Kiyomori died
1185 the Minamoto wiped out the Taira forces
1192 Yoritomo called himself shogun
1199 Yoritomo died
1260 Nichiren predicted the Mongols would attack
1274 Mongols attacked Japan
1333 Godaigo tried to recover the throne
1335 Soseki advised Godaigo to improve relations with China
1467 the Onin War broke out
1573 the Ashikaga shogunate ended

THE ASIAN WORLD, 600–1500

ANSWER KEY

Working with Primary Sources
1. The first one, because it tells of a man who gave up his power and riches to live a spiritual life.
2. War was an uncertain time, bringing danger and unexpected harm. So the poem emphasizes the fragility of life.
3. It is important to live a simple, spiritual life, and be grateful for every moment. Life is precious but not guaranteed to last. All living things are sacred.

CHAPTER 11

Cast of Characters
Yi Songgye: Korean general who founded the Choson dynasty and became known as King T'aejo
Wang Kon: the founder of the kingdom of Koryo in 936
Wonjong: the crown prince who surrendered Korea to the Mongols in 1259
T'aejong: the successor to T'aejo
Sejong: king who took the throne after T'aejong who was considered one of the most accomplished and enlightened monarch in history
Munjong: son of Sejong

Word Bank
1. besieged 2. aristocratic

Word Play
unprecedented; Check students' sentences.

What Happened When?
1231 The Koreans killed an Mongol ambassador.
1258 Korean civil officials killed a Cho'e strongman.
1259 Crown prince Wonjong surrendered to the Mongols.
1273 All resistance to the Mongols ceased.
1388 Yi Songgye refused to follow the King's orders to attack China.
1392 Yi Songgye founded the Choson dynasty.
1403 The first successful metal-type printing machine was built.
1419 T'aejong died and Sejong took the throne.
1420 The Hall of Worthies was established.
1443 A new Korean script was created
1450 Sejong died and Munjong took the throne.

Critical Thinking
1. d; 2. a; 3. e; 4. c; 5. b

Working with Primary Sources
Answers will vary, but should include that T'aejo thought he was the people's choice, but the people thought he rose to the position of king because of his ancestors.

Working with Primary Sources
1. Things happen again and again, with similar causes and effects.
2. Some things happen for the first time ever; this invention is something that was surely never seen before.
3. Quotation I: Time contains events that repeat themselves over and over again; quotation II: Time contains events that happen once, for the first and only time.

CHAPTER 12

Cast of Characters
Zhu Yuanzhang (Ming Taizu): founder and first emperor of the Ming Dynasty
Zhu Di (Yongle): fourth son of Taizu under whose rule China's maritime trade flourished
Zheng He: chief admiral under Yongle who led seven voyages in the Indian Ocean and the South China Sea
Fan Ji: scholar who urged the end to the maritime voyages and an increase in agriculture and education

Word Bank
1. epidemic 2. retaliation 3. regulation

Word Play
prosperous; Check students' sentences.

Critical Thinking
2, 3, 6, 4, 1, 8, 5, 7

Working with Primary Sources
Answers will vary.

Critical Thinking
Taizu: b, f
Yongle: d, e, g
Both: a, c

Working with Primary Sources
1. The first and the third statements are against China reaching out beyond its borders (war burdens the population, and the state does not necessarily benefit from trade with other nations); the second speaker wants trade and interaction with other nations.
2. Each side reflects different attitudes about China's position in the world at that time.